THE GRINGO'S GUIDE TO
IMMIGRATION
REFORM
FOR
EMPLOYERS

WHAT READERS SAID ABOUT *THE GRINGO'S GUIDE TO HISPANICS IN THE WORKPLACE*

"Every chapter is filled with insights on how to get ahead of the curve and take a leadership position. If you don't read this book, then expect your company to miss some golden opportunities."

—William J. Lawrence
Chairman, Bubbles Enterprises LTD.

"Throw away your other books dealing with Hispanics in the workplace. This book is now the definitive guide. Following Jacob's practical advice will reduce turnover, increase productivity and ensure everyone is treated with dignity and respect."

—Michael L. Gooch
SPHR, Author of Wingtips with Spurs

"Essential reading for every employer in the U.S. working with Spanish-speaking employees. A couple hours reading can give you the knowledge that it took me 30 years to learn—the hard way. A must read for human resource managers."

—Mark Smoky Heuston
HR Director, Dakota Provisions

THE GRINGO'S GUIDE TO
IMMIGRATION
REFORM
FOR
EMPLOYERS

BY
JACOB M. MONTY
AND
SARAH D. MONTY-ARNONI

MONTY & RAMIREZ LLP
ATTORNEYS AT LAW

EMPORION PRESS

Emporion Press
www.antaeusbooks.com/emporion

To the Gringos* who have moved immigration reform legislation forward over the past twenty years. They are the reason why comprehensive immigration reform is on the brink of existence. Their tireless efforts against difficult obstacles are heroic.

These Gringos, in business, politics, and academia, keep pushing for reform when the polls and pundits signal another way. They stand with our community and uphold the dream that is America. For that, thank you.

---

*In this book, we use the term "Gringo" to mean all non-immigrant U.S. citizens. Gringos are not just "Anglos," but non-immigrant U.S. citizens of all races and ethnicities.

CONTENTS

ABOUT THE AUTHORS

JACOB M. MONTY serves as managing partner of Houston-headquartered Monty & Ramirez LLP, the largest Hispanic-owned labor and immigration law firm in the U.S.A. He has counseled companies with large Hispanic workforces for 18 years, defending them in lawsuits, investigations by federal and state agencies, and helping them win union elections. He is passionate about defending his clients, ranging from family-owned enterprises to publicly traded companies, and also about the Hispanic worker. The firm has represented thousands of individuals in immigration matters, including routine Deferred Action for Childhood Arrivals (DACA) applications or deportation litigation defense, which keeps families together. He brings a wealth of real-world knowledge to the reader. Professional exploits include defending employers involved in some of the largest raids and investigations by Immigration Customs and Enforcement, and successfully winning for companies some of the most contested union elections. He

has also gone underground, posing as an undocumented immigrant, to expose widespread document counterfeit rings that prey on employers and employees alike. Jacob is a vigorous Latino advocate. His expertise on Latino issues has been sought after by the Bush White House and in many political campaigns, both Republican and Democrat. He was offered the then INS Commissioner position by President George W. Bush in 2001, but chose to stay in private practice. He also organized the first U.S. Department of Labor Latino Safety Summit in Charlotte, North Carolina, in 2004.

SARAH D. MONTY-ARNONI, partner and leader of the immigration practice group for Monty & Ramirez LLP, practices exclusively U.S. immigration and naturalization law counseling employers and employees in all aspects of immigration law including nonimmigrant and immigrant visas, permanent residency, citizenship, and compliance applicable to both U.S. employers and the foreign nationals whom they employ. Her clients include investors, emerging and mid-sized businesses, and large corporations in industries such as energy, health care, IT consulting, oil and gas, financial services, and the import/export of retail goods. Ms. Monty-Arnoni assists clients in performing "immigration due diligence" in preparation for corporate restructures and M&A transactions. She assists foreign nationals at U.S. consulates and embassies abroad to facilitate the issuance of visas necessary to enter the U.S., and represents employers and foreign nationals before the Department of Homeland Security, the Department of State, the Department of Labor, and the Department of Justice. Sarah also brings her immigration horsepower to Monty & Ramirez pro bono clients at no charge. Through her efforts, she has kept families together that would have otherwise been torn apart as a result of deportation. A frequent speaker to business and community groups on immigration, Sarah is also the co-founder and director of Protectors of the Dream, Inc., a 501(c)(3) non-profit organization serving immigrant youth, which has raised thousands of dollars for deserving DACA applicants who lacked the money for the government filing fees. She is a passionate advocate for businesses and immigrants.

PREFACE

The purpose of this book is to guide and inform employers and their friends. We use the word "friends"—meaning your Hispanic employees and associates—to remind you all that until comprehensive immigration reform passes, you must avoid learning that your employees are actually undocumented. Not all Hispanic employees are undocumented, of course, but some may be, and you do not want to acquire that knowledge. An employer must avoid directly learning about employees' work authorization fraud or misrepresentation. Once this knowledge is gained, the employer has a duty to act and terminate the employee.

At some point during the immigration reform process there will be a day when all undocumented people will be required to come forward, and knowledge may be gained without repercussions. Until this day arrives, the employer must avoid having direct knowledge of employee fraud or misrepresentation of work authorization documents.

Meanwhile, Gringo—and we use this common term with respect and friendship for our fellow Americans—employers can be an important voice for comprehensive immigration reform. The number one thing the Gringo needs to do is keep pushing for immigration reform. We invite those reading this book to be a voice for comprehensive immigration reform by contacting your congressional representatives, now. In fact, we're so convinced that your voice matters, we will send a free copy of *The Gringo's Guide to Immigration Reform for Employers*, if you can establish that you've sent a letter or email to your Congressman or Senator and have told five other people to do the same. Please correspond to jmonty@montyramirez.com.

INTRODUCTION
GETTING READY FOR IMMIGRATION REFORM: FOREWARNED IS FOREARMED; "TO BE PREPARED IS HALF THE VICTORY."

"We believe that the cost of doing nothing about our broken immigration system is a far greater threat to the economy than fixing it."

Forewarned is forearmed. Immigration reform is coming. As Miguel de Cervantes writes in Don Quixote, "...*estar preparado es ya media victoria*; to be prepared is half the victory."

Our current immigration system is broken. For one thing, the H1B visa category for highly-skilled employees is not sufficient to meet the needs of U.S. employers. In 2013, the cap in this visa category was reached in April, forcing skilled employees who are frequently educated in top U.S. universities to leave the country and ultimately to compete against U.S. employers.

In addition, employers trying to fill blue collar jobs have to contend with severe labor shortages and audits from ICE. Further, immigrants who fill these ranks live in fear solely because they are working to support their families.

Immigrants who are eligible for family-based visas sometimes wait up to 20 years or more before they can obtain employment authorization. The need for a system that benefits employers, protects U.S. citizens and allows immigrants who are in the U.S., supporting our economy, is long over due!

A comprehensive immigration reform plan, one that creates a path to legalization for unauthorized workers and includes a flexible visa program will not only raise the wage floor for all American workers, but will prove to be an economic necessity. Immigration reform will positively impact employers because it will expand the available workforce and decrease the possibility of hiring unauthorized workers.

Data compiled in a joint report by The Center for American Progress (CAP) and Immigration Policy Center (IPC), "Raising the Floor for American Workers: The Economic Benefits of Comprehensive Immigration Reform," estimates that comprehensive immigration reform stands to grow the U.S. economy by $1.5 trillion over ten years and in the short term, within three years, generate $4.5 to $5.4 billion in additional tax revenue and consumer spending sufficient to support 750,000 to 900,000 jobs.

Several state-level studies show that the increased economic activity created by lower-skilled, mostly Hispanic* immigrants far exceeds the costs to state and local governments. For example, a 2006 study by the Kenan Institute of Private Enterprise at the University of North Carolina at Chapel Hill and reported by the CATO Institute found that the rapidly growing population of Hispanics in the

---

* "Hispanic" and "Latino" will be used interchangeably throughout this book.

state, had contributed $756 million in taxes—directly and indirectly—while providing vital labor to key North Carolina industries.

In addition, the IPC says that deportation would poison the already anemic U.S. economy by draining $2.5 trillion in Gross Domestic Product (GDP) over 10 years, even before factoring in the costs of deporting 12 million people and permanently sealing the border.

Halting all immigration into the United States would explode the size of the national Social Security deficit. The arrival of newcomers is key to funding Social Security for older Americans.

Over the next 75 years, it is projected that immigrants will contribute $611 billion to U.S. Social Security coffers. The independent National Foundation for American Policy claims that halting all immigration into the United States would explode the size of the national Social Security deficit, and that the arrival of newcomers is key to funding Social Security for older Americans, those who are at or near retirement. They estimate at least a 31 percent increase in that deficit in the next 50 years without continued immigration. The Social Security Administration Chief Actuary Stephen Goss acknowledges that undocumented immigrants have contributed $150 billion to the Social Security trust fund without recieving any benefits.

And yet, there is no shortage of anti-immigration rhetoric spewed out on the American public, such as the following:

"When you legalize those who are in the country illegally, it costs taxpayers millions of dollars, costs American workers thousands of jobs and encourages more illegal immigration." *–Republican Representative Lamar Smith, Texas*

"I think we need immigration reform. But I do think that they have to deal with the welfare situation. Because if you're going to add another six million people, and, believe me, when welfare gets—when welfare, when immigration reform gets passed, that means the people that are in the other countries are going to be able to come here." *–News Entertainer Bill O'Reilly*

If only it were that simple. The nativists often cite a study released in August 2012 by The Center for Immigration Studies, an anti-immigration group. Their study reports that 39 percent of households led by native-born Americans with children used welfare programs, specifically food assistance and Medicaid, compared to 57 percent of households headed by undocumented immigrants, who themselves do not qualify for government assistance but whose U.S.-born children and spouses can receive assistance such as free school lunches, food stamps, public housing, and rent subsidies.

However, the reality is that the vast majority of immigrants, both documented and undocumented, contribute more to this country than they take out in social services. And the cost of doing nothing about a broken immigration system is the far greater threat to our economy. Immigration reform is imminent. If the proposals on the table haven't impacted your business yet, they will when it is passed. Employers need to remain informed and BE PREPARED.

Forewarning and forearming you, *The Gringo's Guide to Immigration Reform* was written to do just that: Prepare employers for new requirements in compliance, documentation and employer-employee relations. The guide is designed to help you, the employer, counteract undue union pressure and manage healthcare benefits under ObamaCare. This guide will also equip Gringo readers with essential information that they can share with "friends" that are seeking help, hope and ways to make their dreams reality.

In the words of the Honorable Senator from South Carolina, Lindsey Graham, "I hope the third time is the charm."

WARNING! ¡CUIDADO!

If an employee asks you about reform before it passes, tread carefully but confidentially with these caveats:

- *"I assume you are asking on behalf of a friend or family member. Please refer that person to this attorney."*
- Avoid letting the employee tell you she needs help with reform for herself.
- Avoid asking the employee if she needs help.
- Remember, millions of undocumented people are married to U.S. citizens and/or residents, so your employee could plausibly be asking on behalf of a friend or family member.

THE GRINGO'S GUIDE TO
IMMIGRATION
REFORM
FOR
EMPLOYERS

CHAPTER 1
LA NETA (THE TRUTH): KNOWLEDGE IS POWER FOR YOU AND YOUR EMPLOYEES

> *"Let's start that conversation by acknowledging we aren't going to deport 12 million illegal immigrants. If you wish to work, if you wish to live and work in America, then we will find a place for you."*
>
> —Kentucky Senator Rand Paul
> (March 19, 2013)

Employers need to be acutely aware about the developing details of immigration reform. Employers must be diligent about staying informed because employees will likely go to their employers for answers to their questions. Your information, or lack thereof, is pivotal in nurturing a stable workforce.

Keep in mind that Hispanic workers often identify emotionally with the company they work for and look to company leaders for trusted information on a range of issues. As stated in our previous book, *The Gringo's Guide to Hispanics in the Workplace*:

"Hispanic immigrants often come from countries where the identity of a company's founder is celebrated and cherished in the workplace. They tend to value knowing who the founder and key managers are so they can identify personally with them and talk about their accomplishments with family and friends. After all, Mexican and Central American cultures tend to place a great deal of importance on hierarchy and class."

Similarly, your employees often look to you for solid information on immigration issues. To understand the need and hunger of such information, look no further than Spanish media.

Univision, a popular Spanish-language television network dedicated to providing programming for Latin American families who reside in the United States, has the largest audience of Spanish-language television viewers in the world, according to Nielsen ratings. In recent years the network has reached parity with the five major U.S. English-language television networks. As of 2012, Univision gained first-place rankings for individual programs over all five English-language networks, all 52 weeks of the year.

Leveraging the energy created by immigration reform in order to attract viewers, Univision frequently broadcasts content such as "¡Reforma Migratoria Ahora! Immigration Reform Now!" on their newscasts. The emotions stirred up by these programs cause ratings to increase because viewers stay tuned to learn about new developments in immigration reform. Hispanic immigrants are anxious to learn about changes in immigration reform, and Univision is quick to answer the call.

IMMIGRATION REFORM PRESENTS A HUGE OPPORTUNITY FOR EMPLOYERS

By keeping abreast of immigration developments, you demonstrate to your Hispanic workforce that you are concerned with matters affecting them. You will also find that a common factor such as immigration reform that links company well-being to worker well-being compels a diverse workforce to work together for the collective benefit of the company. When an employer establishes that it has its employees' best interests in mind, the employer creates a more loyal and unified work environment and builds respect for the organization.

Conversely, an employer's failure to stay informed and communicate with its workforce provides an opening for unions and others to influence employees – to the detriment of the employer. Although it may take a great deal of effort to sift through the political rhetoric to determine what's really going on in immigration reform, your efforts will be well worth it in the long run.

> *Legislation is only a starting point for immigration reform. Expect lengthy committee hearings and debates.*

The major news outlets report daily on various debates, proposals, and progress of immigration reform. While some reports seem slanted to support particular positions, if you collect your information from a variety of sources, you will acquire a good understanding of the central issues. How to even begin educating yourself about immigration reform may be difficult. A simple Internet search on immigration reform produces hundreds of informative articles—some with up-to-the minute coverage. In our offices, we have a Google Alert set for certain immigration reform topics. The alert notifies us of updates via an email with links to news articles and blog commentary on each topic of which we wish to keep abreast. We also advise you to add the Department of Homeland Security (DHS) website (www. dhs.gov) and the U.S. Customs & Immigration Services (USCIS) website (www.uscis.gov) to your favorites and to peruse them frequently, especially the news and updates pages. If you are not already familiar with these websites, it is crucial that you take time to familiarize yourself with them right now.

We understand that the amount of information before you may be intimidating, but you cannot afford to not be informed. Before you begin to inundate yourself with information about immigration reform, take note that you are preparing for the future, as immigration reform may still be a long way away. Before the President even has the opportunity to sign immigration reform into law, parties in both houses of Congress must agree to and approve of the terms of the reform – no simple task.

Between now and the day when immigration reform becomes law and meaningful implementation occurs, there are a myriad of issues impacting employees and employers and their relationship with each other—for better or worse. Your employees will seek answers, and you cannot afford to be in the dark. You must be informed.

UNDERSTANDING THE GANG OF EIGHT'S
BIPARTISAN PROPOSAL

"First of all, Americans support it in poll after poll. Secondly, Latino voters expect it. Third, Democrats want it. And fourth, Republicans need it." —Senator Bob Menendez of New Jersey, one of four Democrats in the bipartisan "Gang of Eight"

Understanding the future of immigration requires acquainting yourself with a group of Senators known as the "Gang of Eight." These eight legislators, comprised of both Democrats and Republicans, are leading a non-partisan immigration law overhaul in Senate. The last comprehensive revision of the nation's immigration law came in 1986, and the Gang of Eight is steadfastly working toward the next comprehensive revision.

Under the initial proposal presented by the Gang of Eight, the 11 million undocumented immigrants already in the U.S. would be eligible for probationary legal status allowing them to lawfully work if they register with the government and pay a fine. The plan would not give permanent legal status, however, until measures are taken to address the flow of undocumented immigrants across U.S. borders. Undocumented immigrants who come clean under comprehensive immigration reform will not receive special treatment. In fact, it will be very tough. The Gang of Eight's proposal puts newly legalized immigrants at the back of the line for green cards and excludes them from receiving any federal benefits such as food stamps, Medicare, or welfare while waiting. Under the plan, the time between when an individual acquires lawful permanent residency and when the individual is eligible for citizenship will be extended significantly.

IMMIGRATION REFORM'S MAIN TENANTS

Immigration reform under the Gang of Eight's proposal would create a "tough but fair" path to citizenship for undocumented immigrants currently living in the U.S., contingent upon the government screening the U.S. borders. The plan also proposes to streamline the legal immigration system and create incentives to lure sought-after tech and science wizzes, working, in essence, to build the American economy and strengthen families. Further, the plan would require all employers to use E-Verify to verify the immigration status of potential hires and to prevent identity theft and the hiring of unauthorized workers. Finally, it proposes to create ways for employers—particularly in the agricultural sector—to find low-wage guest workers when American workers are not available.

LIFTING THE SHADOW OF DEPORTATION FROM YOUNG, HARDWORKING PEOPLE

> *"There are an estimated 11.5 million people like me in this country, human beings with stories as varied as America itself yet lacking a legal claim to exist here."*
> —*journalist Jose Antonio Vargas*

In 2001, Senators Dick Durbin and Orrin Hatch proposed legislation centered around the argument that it makes no sense to remove hardworking young people who were brought to this country through no fault of their own and who have grown up in the United States, often with no memory of the countries they came from. The "DREAM Act" (Development, Relief, and Education for Alien Minors) would qualify undocumented youth to be eligible for a 6-year long conditional path to citizenship and require the completion of a college degree or two years of military service.

However, in June 2012, the DHS and President Obama, under pressure from Hispanic voters and others who said he hadn't fulfilled a 2008 campaign promise to overhaul the tangled U.S. immigration laws, announced a new executive "exercise in discretion" to allow certain young people who were brought to the U.S. as young children to obtain deferment from deportation (for two years) and receive temporary work-authorization. The hurdles for obtaining this deferment for deportation are high, and only those who meet several key criteria are eligible to apply. This exercise of discretion did not create a formal law, but is called a "Deferred Action for Childhood Arrivals," known by the acronym DACA. DACA is a good preview of how comprehensive immigration reform will change lives on a larger scale.

DACA ESSENTIALS

The USCIS formally launched DACA on August 15, 2012. DACA is neither a path to citizenship nor a permanent fix to immigration issues, as only Congress can provide a permanent fix through comprehensive immigration reform. And, while we know immigration reform will be passed eventually, we do not know when it will be passed, and it may be months or even years before practical implementation can be felt and impact on employers realized. The immediate importance of DACA cannot be underestimated, and employers must be familiar with its provisions.

DACA provides that individuals under the age of 31 as of June 15, 2012, may be eligible for relief from deportation and may be granted temporary work authorization if they meet the following criteria:

(1) The individual must have arrived in the United States before reaching their 16th birthday.

(2) The individual must prove continuous residency in the United States from June 15, 2007, to the present time.

(3) The individual must have been physically present in the United States on June 15, 2012, and at the time of making the request for a deferred action.

(4) The individual must prove that they entered without inspection before June 15, 2012, or that their lawful immigration status expired before June 15, 2012.

(5) The individual must be enrolled in school (primary, secondary, college, or trade school) or have a diploma from a high school or college or a Certificate of Completion from high school such as a General Education Development (GED) Certificate. Alternately, proof that they are an honorably discharged veteran of the Coast Guard or Armed Forces of the United States is accepted.

(6) DACA applicants must not have a felony, a significant misdemeanor, or three or more other misdemeanors.

(7) The individual must pass through a database inspection and be proven to not otherwise pose a threat to national security or public safety. (See also Chapter 9.)

If the DHS exercises its discretion and grants deferred action to an individual, the individual is then eligible to obtain a work permit and, under limited circumstances, may also obtain permission to travel in and out of the U.S.

WHAT DACA MEANS TO EMPLOYERS

DHS spokespersons have assured the public that the agency is not interested in investigating DACA applications for the purpose of prosecuting employers unless there appears to be a "widespread pattern and practice of unlawful hiring" by a particular employer. Be advised that this statement is not necessarily bulletproof. In fact, business owners and CEOs have been quoted in the press, including The New York Times, as saying that these government statements do not reassure them.

As an employer, you may have your share of younger workers, and if so, it is especially important that you pay attention to DACA and are well versed in its provisions. Within a young workforce, the likelihood of one successful DACA applicant turning into many successful DACA applicants is entirely possible. If this happens, there are some questions that you must be prepared to answer.

PROVING CONTINUOUS RESIDENCY

As noted in criteria number two above, DACA applicants must prove continuous residency in the United States.

While there are several ways an individual can demonstrate continuous residency, one option is to provide a letter from their employer documenting their work dates. Employers need to be acutely aware that how they respond to requests for employment documentation in any regard can cause problems—such as actual or constructive knowledge of illegal work status—if not handled correctly.

As there are a number of circumstances where an employee will ask for employment verification, having a neutral company policy regarding all requests for letters stating dates of employment will save you some really big headaches. DACA applicants can prove continuous residency through several types of documents. Our clients have used

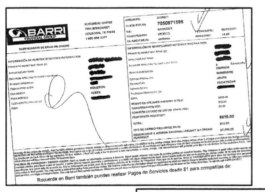

Receipts from remittance services can help DACA applicants prove continuous residency.

school records, phone bills and receipts from remittance services. Employer letters are not required but may be used.

(For a complete discussion of how and why employers should create an employee policy for employment verification letters, see Chapter 8.)

CHAPTER 2
CAUTION: THE FEDS ARE COMING TO ENFORCE WAGE LAWS

"Company pay practices are under greater scrutiny than ever before...."

A California tech firm contracted 14 Mexican nationals to work on the company's generators between November 2010 and November 2012. The group, which was brought in on visitor visas, was paid in pesos—paychecks were deposited to bank accounts in Mexico—at the equivalent of $2.66 an hour. The federal minimum wage at that time was $7.25 per hour. After the U.S. Department of Labor (DOL) investigated the site and uncovered this fact, the U.S. District Court judge ordered the company to pay the group $31,922 in both back wages and damages. The company was also fined another $6,160 in damages by the DOL.

A NEWLY EMPOWERED WORKFORCE

Typically, your immigrant employees come from civil law countries where the courts do not play a strong role in protecting the rights of the citizens as they do in our common law system,

*and class action law suits are virtually unheard of. On top of
that, undocumented workers are often unaware of their rights
in our judicial system or just plain scared to use them. Nevertheless, two of the strongest motivating factors for immigrants to
leave their countries of origin are the prospects of making more
money and safety. It would be naïve for an employer with bad
pay practices to think that a newly documented workforce will
not take advantage of all of the rights and protections that come
with their new status.*

WAGE AND HOUR ENFORCEMENT CRACKDOWN

Statistically, the DOL wage and hour enforcement under the
Obama administration has become markedly more hostile
toward employers. For example, the number of "directed"
investigations—those not initiated by an employee complaint—increased by nine percent between 2008 and 2011
and now comprises 32 percent of all DOL investigations.
They are conducting more unannounced investigations into
businesses without any prior record of violations. Further,
investigators are being instructed to seek civil penalties. Finally, they are giving employers less time to respond, threatening subpoena actions in federal court against employers
who fail to respond in a timely manner.

The DOL's Wage and Hour Division (WHD) has an
increased enforcement budget for 2013 and has hired 350
new investigators over the last two years, seeking to total
1,839 full-time investigators—50 percent more federal
wage and hour investigators than in 2008. This increased

workforce of investigators impacts employers in several new ways. One, for example, being that investigations formerly resolved at a single site are now frequently escalated to an enterprise-wide basis. Another example is the re-prioritization of industry-wide targets. In 2012, the WHD conducted more than 100 investigations as part of a multi-year enforcement initiative specifically focused on Fair Labor Standards Act (FLSA) compliance among New Jersey gas stations and recovered more than $2.3 million in back wages for more than 500 gas station workers. FLSA fines are an easy way to generate needed money for the government with a growing federal deficit. It is unlikely that these investigations will stop anytime soon.

ASTOUNDING RECOVERIES

To give you a sense of just how aggressive the investigations have become in just the first two months of 2013, here are some eye-popping FLSA recoveries:

$3M – gas station enterprise – New Jersey
$78,000 – landscaping company – New Jersey
$424,000 – restaurant group – Massachusetts
$89,000 – landscaping company – New Jersey
$1.3M – directory assistance provider – Pennsylvania
$17,000 – accounting firm – Virginia
$1 million – restaurant group – New York
$39,000 – printing company – Georgia
$226,000 – painting contractor – Southeast
$90,000 – agricultural employer – Florida
$758,000 – golf course company – North Carolina

$365,000 – agricultural employer– Florida
$59,000 – racing stables – Kentucky
$232,000 – supermarkets – Ohio
$92,000 – manufacturer – Kansas
$216,000 – tires and auto service – Iowa
$17,000 – dry-cleaning business – Wisconsin
$97,000 – sportswear company – Kansas
$16,000 – retailer – Kansas
$56,000 – jewelry manufacturer – Oklahoma
$44,000 – software company – Texas
$184,000 – chemical provider – Pennsylvania
$76,000 – commercial construction products – Texas
$100,000 – coffee producer – Hawaii
$120,000 – insurance services - California

If these numbers aren't enough to motivate employers to take the FLSA requirements seriously, keep in mind that the government can enforce *criminal* penalties against employers who have willfully violated the law. Do not think that you will not get caught, or that you will get a pass on your first-time offense. The odds of that these days are slim.

LOW HANGING FRUIT FOR ICE AND DHS

The Department of Homeland Security (DHS) and Immigration & Customs Enforcement (ICE) will conduct an investigation if they find cause—regardless of business size, type or location. But, if your company falls into one the traditionally "low wage industries" you are considered one of the agencies' three top priorities.

According to the DOL, the following industries are flush with minimum wage employees, have high rates of violations, are typically comprised of vulnerable employees less likely to complain if not paid as required under the FLSA, and show rapid growth and decline of businesses:

- garment;
- agriculture;
- health care;
- day care;
- restaurants;
- hospitality;
- guard services;
- janitorial;
- landscaping; and
- temporary help.

While all companies are required by law to maintain consistency with the FLSA, a company in any of the above industries will need to be especially careful with processes, pay rates, and record keeping in order to stay in compliance. Keep in mind that these days the DOL does not always work alone! A compliance issue that is discovered in the investigation of one agency can turn into an investigation by the other agency, as well.

More recently, the DOL has a memorandum of understanding with ICE to work together, which has led to increased investigations. In addition to working with ICE, the DOL has teamed up with the IRS to audit companies that are using independent contractors. These two agencies are working together to shore up the loophole and collect otherwise lost tax-revenue for the government.

WAGE AND HOUR CLAIMS GROW

Plaintiffs (employees) today bring more than three and a half times as many FLSA cases as they did 10 years ago, when the annual court filings for the year ending March 31, 2001, totaled only 1,961 cases. From April 1, 2010 through March 31, 2011, plaintiffs filed 7,008 FLSA cases in federal courts. This represents *an increase of more than 15 percent* over the prior year.

The lawsuits filed by your employees or former employees for violating the FLSA can be far more costly than the fines imposed by the DOL. A New York court approved a settlement of $42 million against J.P. Morgan who mistakenly classified underwriters as managers, thereby failing to pay the required overtime wages. Class members in this suit may receive as much as $94,000 each. In California and Maryland plaintiffs have filed FLSA and state-wage law violations simultaneously, thereby increasing their settlement amounts anywhere from $2.7 million to $14.1 million such as in the case of Starbuck's who mistakenly allowed their shift supervisors to share in the tip jars.

In addition, courts are now frequently giving plaintiff lawyers extra time to find class action plaintiffs in cases where the class includes Spanish speakers and employees who may have moved to other states or countries, increasing the cost of these suits by increasing the size of the class. Unfortunately, these figures do not include the fees paid in defending these lawsuits. On top of that, judgments are printed in newspapers, both offline and online, affecting the public opinion of the companies being sued by their employees for pay violations.

UNDOCUMENTED WORKERS CAN FILE FLSA CLAIMS

The courts have been clear that undocumented workers are "employees" under the FLSA and they can file suits receiving back wages, liquidated damages (doubling of back pay), and attorneys' fees. Although undocumented workers currently have the right to file FLSA lawsuits, many of them are simply afraid to use the courts. However, going forward, you should expect that newly documented workers in the wake of immigration reform will likely not hesitate to exercise their rights once they have the protection of work authorization.

Currently, there are some industries that seem to be vulnerable to FLSA lawsuits. Industries targeted in FLSA class actions and WHD investigations include:

- construction, specifically residential construction;
- hospitality, specifically food/beverage and house-keeping;
- janitorial;
- home health care;
- child care;
- transportation;
- warehousing;
- meat/poultry processing;

- staffing companies;
- franchisor/franchisee; and
- corporate parent/subsidiary.

WHAT YOU NEED TO DO NOW

Now more than ever, companies need to make wage and hour compliance a priority. It is imperative that you make sure that your wage and hour compliance program meets the DOL's standards. Once you are sure that pay policies and practices comply with both federal and state law, you must train your employees, especially managers.

Ignoring these two steps, compliance audits and training, are where companies are most likely to fail in compliance programs—either the program is flawed from the beginning or they fail to communicate it to mid-level managers who supervise employees and implement the program. But companies that complete those two steps and implement a program to test their compliance periodically find that FLSA compliance is cheaper than the back pay and fines imposed by the government or a costly lawsuit. A program that includes training and testing shows good faith.

BEST PRACTICES: CONDUCT AN FLSA AUDIT

We cannot implore employers enough regarding the importance of conducting an internal audit for FLSA compliance. Considering the risks and costs that you potentially face if you do not conduct an audit, conducting an audit should be a no-brainer. Moreover, the process is very simple.

The first step is to identify the employees in exempt positions and verify that those employees are indeed exempt from overtime. Generally, the most common are the executive exemption and the administrative exemption. We encourage you to familiarize yourself with all of the exemptions, and a good place to start is the DOL Factsheet regarding exemptions, accessible at http://www.dol.gov/whd/regs/compliance/fairpay/fs17a_overview.pdf.

The second step is to identify your hourly employees who are eligible for overtime. Regarding these hourly employees, you must audit your records, policies, and practices to ensure that your hourly employees are being paid properly. Again, the DOL website is an excellent place to start looking for guidance to be compliant with the FLSA.

Employee Records. Every human resource professional in your organization, no matter what their role or specialty, should be familiar with the exact information that the company is required to keep for every employee under the FLSA. If you haven't audited your personnel files in the past year, it is time to do so. Ensure that the following information is complete and up-to-date:

- employee's full name, as used for Social Security purposes, and on the same record, the employee's identifying symbol or number if such is used in place of name on any time, work, or payroll records;
- address, including zip code;
- birth date, if younger than 19;
- occupation;
- time and day of week when employee's workweek begins, hours worked each day, and total hours worked each workweek;
- basis on which employee's wages are paid;

- regular hourly pay rate;
- total daily or weekly straight-time earnings;
- total overtime earnings for the workweek;
- all additions to or deductions from the employee's wages;
- total wages paid each pay period; and
- date of payment and the pay period covered by the payment.

Wage and Hour Policies. In addition to posting official wage and hour materials in your break room or near your time clock, a comprehensive wage and hour policy and a description of remedies should be included in your employee handbook. A comprehensive set would include:

- overtime policy;
- meal and rest break policy;
- tip pool policy (if applicable);
- paid time off or vacation policy (if offered);
- policy prohibiting off the clock work that also identifies activities that are considered compensable work such as sending emails at home, working during meal periods and travel time;
- policy prohibiting employees from entering inaccurate time; and
- a process for filing complaints and internal investigations.

Policy and Training Maintenance for Managers. In the daily grind of keeping up with the laws that apply to non-exempt employees, especially where there is high turn-over, it's often easy to overlook the needs of exempt employees. All managers—*exempt employees*—need be trained on wage and hour issues. It is especially important to offer training immediately upon an employee's promotion to manager, and also on a regular basis thereafter.

In our experience, it is not enough to hand a new manager a stack of information and expect them to fully comprehend the material, let alone have the free time to do so. In areas like FLSA, where the stakes are high, it is important to schedule a mandatory training and review session annually. Further, you might consider establishing a mentor/mentee program that pairs a senior manager or human resource professional with a new or junior manager and require a weekly or monthly meeting where they can openly discuss any questions or issues.

Managers need to be fluent in all company policies, but in particular, those that have technical requirements such as FLSA. Managers are the company representatives, interacting day-to-day with employees. They have to understand the liability created by changing time slips, allowing employees to work "off the clock" for only tips, not paying overtime, not allowing employees to take protected leave, or any wage and hour issue that is unique to your industry and your newly empowered, documented workforce.

FLSA lawsuits and DOL investigations can be avoided with fair pay practices and good record keeping. A great compliance program will start with a solid policy, continue with great training, and end with periodic testing to ensure that it is working properly. Now—before immigration reform happens—is the time to redouble your FLSA compliance efforts so that when reform comes you can enjoy its benefits and not face an extensive DOL audit or class action lawsuit.

Chapter 3

"AHORA ME LLAMO JACOBO": WHAT HAPPENS WHEN UNDOCUMENTED JUAN BECOMES DOCUMENTED JACOBO?

A simple, legal change of name, for instance through marriage, is easy to explain. But when an employee informs you that their name, date of birth, or social security number is substantially different from that which was previously used to complete his or her Form I-9, and they are unable to provide evidence linking the new information to the previous identity, it's a "Catch 22" for the employer. Do you (a) fire him or her because he or she lied about prior documentation or (b) keep the employee now that he or she has legal authorization?

While there is no "duty" to fire an employee who reveals that they were originally hired under a false identity, Immigration and Customs Enforcement (ICE) agents have been known to use evidence of a company's lax practice of allowing employees to change identities as grounds for prosecution.

From a strictly business standpoint, it may seem economical and efficient to keep the employee since the company has already invested in the employee's training and values their experience. However, this does not address the serious issue that the employee was dishonest and intentionally broke the law.

PREPARE TODAY FOR THE EFFECTS OF REFORM

Companies are facing this name change dilemma more frequently today, as immigrants who were previously working without documentation are being granted work authorization through the Presidential mandate, Deferred Action for Childhood Arrivals (DACA). Employers who did not know that their employees were working with false identification or false authorization are making decisions on the fly about how to respond to this situation. If you prepare today you can assess what terms, if any, you will allow employees to remain on your payroll.

STANDARD POLICY

You cannot be charged with a verification violation if you have a good faith defense against the imposition of employer sanctions and penalties for knowingly hiring an unauthorized individual, unless the government can show you had knowledge of the unauthorized status of the employee. Still, a standard policy for handling dishonesty in the workplace is a wise and proactive tool for all employers.

A standard policy should provide the company full discretion in treating all lying, including resume fraud and false identity, as a basis for termination. One policy option is to accept newly confirmed authorized identities from employees that volunteer this information and reject those who come up with a new identity only when confronted with problems about the current identity. For example, some companies may choose to excuse employees who are forthcoming with their mistakes in order to encourage honesty in the workplace.

NAME CHANGE AND FORM I-9

While employers are not required to update Form I-9 when an employee has a legal change of name, we always advise that is best to maintain correct information on I-9s. If you find an unverifiable name change, it may call into question your continued ability to rely on the previously submitted documents and avoid being hit with fines if you are audited.

There are some steps you can take to be reasonably assured of the employee's identity, the accuracy of any legal name change, and whether or not the identity change merits a new Form I-9 for your records. But, if your employee informs you that their name, date of birth, or Social Security number is substantially different from that previously provided on Form I-9 and is unable to provide evidence linking the new information to the identity previously used you should definitely complete a new Form I-9.

On the new I-9, write the original hire date in "The employee's first day of employment (MM/DD/YYYY)" space and attach the new Form I-9 to the previously completed Form I-9.

A responsible employer will take a little extra attentiveness when an employee brings in a new name, social security card or work authorization. If the Section 1 information (that is filled out by the employee and documents identity) has not substantially changed but the employee has offered different evidence of work authorization, then you should examine the documentation to determine if it appears to be genuine as it relates to the employee presenting it. Due diligence is the key here. Any document brought in that creates a new identity needs to be carefully verified.

If work authorization has changed and been verified, the employer should complete Section 3 of the previous Form I-9 noting any explanation, and likewise for the name change. This will clearly document your actions in the event that the government asks to inspect your I-9 forms.

If you do complete a new I-9, always keep the previous I-9 with the current I-9 to show the company's good faith effort to comply with the guidelines.

The M-274 Handbook found on the U.S. Customs and Immigration Service (USCIS) website is your best resource for updated guidance on recording changes of name and other identity guidance.

USCIS RECOMMENDATIONS

As stated above, employers are not required to update Form I-9 when an employee changes his or her name. However, USCIS recommends that you maintain correct information on Forms I-9 and note any name changes in Section 3. Further, Form I-9 regulations do not require that an employee present you with any new documentation to show that they he or she has changed their name. However, you may take steps—such as asking the employee for the basis of the name change—to be reasonably assured of the employee's identity and the veracity of the employee's claim of a name change.

When to complete a Form I-9 for existing employees

If any of the information has changed in Section 1 of the previously completed Form I-9:	• Employee's name • Date of birth • Attestation • SSN, if previously provided	Then an employer should: • Complete a new Form I-9	• Write original hire date in Section 2 • Attach new Form I-9 to previously completed I-9

When to complete Section 3 for existing employees

If, after review of the previously completed I-9, the employer finds: • The information in Section	1 has not changed, and • The employee presents a new EAD	Then an employer should: • Examine the documentation to determine if it appears to be genuine and to relate to	the employee presenting it. Record the doc title, number, and expiration date, if any. • Sign and date Section 3.

If the employer previously completed Section 3, or if the version of the form the employer used for a previous verification is no longer valid, the employer must complete Section 3 of the new Form I-9 using the most current version and attach it to the previously completed Form I-9.

If provided by the employee, you may accept a copy of the evidence of the name change to keep with his or her Form I-9 so that your actions are well documented should the government ever ask to inspect your Forms I-9.

PLANNING FOR EMPLOYEE BENEFITS

Most companies were not thinking about immigration reform when they were choosing providers for their benefits programs. More than likely, they were considering things like premiums, benefits to employees, and the cost to the company. Nevertheless, if you choose to hold on to your employees through the immigration reform process, they are likely valued members of your team. Unfortunately, not all providers are concerned about their client's opinion.

Insurance plan administrators have been using the immigration status of employees to deny benefits with varying success. An Iowa court found the plan administrator from Great-West Life and Annuity Insurance Company to have acted **unreasonably** in denying life insurance benefits to the father of an undocumented employee who had falsified his identification in his insurance policy and subsequently hanged himself. There was evidence that company officials had written letters stating their belief that the employee had hanged himself, that the employee was indeed the employee referenced in the insurance policy, and that other employees had taken a collection for the funeral costs. Nevertheless, the employee's identity could not be verified, and Great-West Life and Annuity Insurance Company denied the claim.

In another case, American United Life Insurance was successful in the Eastern District of Texas in denying benefits to an employee's family based on the argument that the application was not filled out truthfully and that the insured had worked and qualified for the plan illegally. In fact, this company testified that it had previously denied benefits 11 times based on these same grounds.

In preparing for immigration reform, we recommend that employers investigate whether or not your benefits providers will support your employees in the same manner that you have. If you provide a name change for a 15 or 20-year old employee, will your provider drop their coverage and make them re-enroll after a 90-day waiting period? If so, is that insurance company the right partner for your company?

CHAPTER 4
EMPLOYEE LOANS: A NECESSARY EVIL
(BUT NOT NECESSARILY EVIL)

"Every year Jim Fab, the owner of an electrical contract-
ing company in Maryland, lends his 25 employees up to
$4,000 interest-free for personal expenses, ranging from
down payments on homes and cars to funeral and legal fees.
Most pay him back — eventually."

According to the *Wall Street Journal Online* article, "Need a Loan? Ask the Boss" (June 4, 2010), one of Mr. Fab's employees dutifully repaid $300 a month for three years after he quit his job. Mr. Fab is not the only employer giving loans to employees. Many business owners do it with little hesitation despite the obvious gamble that they may never see their money again. While the saying "No good deed goes unpunished" too often holds true, that need not be the case. The savvy employer—particularly one with an immigrant workforce— should seriously consider the many benefits of offering company loans to employees, but should also pause to implement a proper policy so as to prevent the potentially costly pitfalls discussed within this chapter.

COMPANY LOANS: A SMALL BUSINESS EMPLOYEE BENEFIT

At small, closely-knit companies, an employer may choose to assume the role of a parent who, for example, opens up the wallet when the kids need cash. This practice is sometimes considered a type of *employee benefit* or substitute for the lack of resources a small company can offer, such as credit unions or debt counseling programs. And it often makes good business sense. It can help prevent a slowdown in productivity from a worker who is stressed out about the money they need for an unexpected emergency or essential purchase. When an employer helps an employee overcome a financial hardship, the employer boosts loyalty, morale and even unity within the workforce. In addition to helping the workforce in general, such loans can eliminate the tangible (and psychological) loss incurred by an employee who has to pay exorbitant fees if faced with no choice but to resort to a loan shark or *prestamista*.

But in some cases, if not handled properly, the benefits of loaning money to an employee can be outweighed by potential problems. Therefore, you should have a policy.

Although all employees may look to their employers to help them in times of financial struggle, Hispanics in particular are accustomed to going to the employer for emergency expenses they cannot cover—illnesses, bail money for family or friends in trouble, and even IMMIGRATION filing fees and lawyer fees. Of course, you might decide that it is best to never loan money to your employees. But you do this at the risk of losing the loyalty of your valued Hispanic workers, many who are managing finances on a minimum wage and expect it from you. *Not* providing loans is *not* always the best policy.

MARIA'S MISTAKE

When her father became unemployed, Maria, almost 26 years old, began supporting her family by working (undocumented) for a national restaurant chain. For almost a year, Maria and her family lived paycheck to paycheck with not a penny left to save for emergencies. Maria had little hope that her father, also an undocumented immigrant, could obtain regular employment, or that she could increase her own earning potential to help her family get ahead. In addition to worrying about financial struggles, Maria's fear of getting caught working illegally and being deported heavily burdened her mind.

Through her co-workers, Maria learned that she might be able to acquire work authorization and be eligible for relief from deportation by filing an application under the Deferred Action for Childhood Arrivals program (DACA), a program recently initiated by the U.S. government in advance of the Dream Act for immigration reform. Maria learned that the DACA application-filing fee was $465 and that if she got the help of a lawyer—at an additional expense—she might be able to expedite the process. Maria estimated she'd need approximately $1000.

Believing that her improved status would open a door to a better paycheck, Maria spoke to a variety of people about getting a loan. With no success, she turned to her employer to ask about a company loan. She promised to pay it back, a little at a time, and even suggested that repayments be deducted from her paychecks. Maria naïvely revealed to her employer what the money was for, unknowingly jeopardizing the future of her employment and her family.

A COMMON PREDICAMENT

Maria's problem is not unique. Millions of individuals in the American workforce face a similar predicament: How is an undocumented laborer surviving on minimum wage expected to save the necessary cash to become work authorized? Consider the expenses faced by individuals in Maria's situation applying for green card —Lawful Permanent Residency:

- Application fee: Up to $1,500 per person
- Penalty fee: $1,000 per head of household; $500 per additional family member
- State impact assistant fee: $500 per head of household
- Renewal fee (every four years): Up to $1,500 per person
- Final penalty before green card: $4,000 per head of household

These fees were part of the 2007 immigration reform proposal. However, the Gang of Eight proposal allows that the Secretary of the Department of Homeland Security (DHS) can set the filing fees for the new applications. The fee will be set to recover the costs of adjudicating filing fees, background checks and fingerprinting. The proposal authorizes the Secretary to limit fees based on family applications, but there is no guarantee that they will be limited. The proposal also includes a mandate that all federal tax liability is settled, and that immigrants over 21 pay a penalty of $1,000. Finally, there is an initial penalty of $500, a renewal penalty of $500 in six years, and a final $1,000 penalty at the end of the provisional period.

There are similar provisions for the application that an immigrant will need to apply for U.S. citizenship. There is also a requirement that immigrants prove that they will not become public charges and that they are at or above 125% of the federal poverty guideline, per household. Meanwhile, the U.S. House of Representatives is working on their own proposal, but it seems likely that filing fees will be high, based on an effort to pay for this overhaul to the immigration system.

So what should Maria have done? Continue to work unlawfully, risk deportation and live in fear? Or look for cash to help solve the problem?

Many undocumented laborers are going to look for cash to solve the problem, and their need for cash puts them in a particularly vulnerable position. Because undocumented laborers have little to no bargaining power and are susceptible to intimidation due to their fear of deportation, they are easy prey for title lenders, loan sharks and the like. Employers of laborers such as Maria have a distinct opportunity for heroism and to create loyalty. We advise employers to be the hero—loan the cash, and help your worker. Nevertheless, be advised that there are issues an employer must consider before deciding whether or not to grant an employee a loan.

COMPANY RESPONSE

Because Maria disclosed to her employer the reason she needed the money, Maria gave her employer knowledge of her undocumented status. Under the current law, with this knowledge, Maria's employer is obligated to terminate her employment. While we're not suggesting that an employer create a policy to enable undocumented workers to work, we are suggesting that if a company has an established neutral loan policy with stated conditions and terms, valuable employees like Maria—who through no fault of their own except that their parents brought them across the border—might today hold the proper work authorization and no longer live in fear.

When immigration reform passes, employers can learn the exact reason employees like Maria need a loan without worrying about the repercussions of such knowledge. Until that day comes, employers should not ask the reason for the loan. Employees should only affirm that the loan is for a life emergency—nothing more. Just as the communication restrictions of "Don't Ask Don't Tell" were eventually repealed, one day soon, immigration laws will be reformed, and reform will permit employers and employees to have honest and candid conversations about issues such as immigration status. Until that time, however, regardless of whether you agree to be a source of emergency money for your workforce, understand that employees will come calling. Be prepared. Have a policy in place.

CONSIDERATIONS WHEN ESTABLISHING A LOAN POLICY

Frankly, if you have a large Hispanic workforce, you are likely already offering company loans to valued employees. If not, ignoring the demand is dangerous since some employees are easy prey to title loan operators, loan sharks, or fraudulent *tandas*. A tanda is an informal banking deal—a form of rotating credit association—among a group of people, sometimes strangers, who contribute their hard earned money to a pot. Participants expect to receive the tanda amount on their given date. Tanda participation requires no identification or interest agreement in advance. A tanda is based purely on trust. Most Latinos have grown up knowing, but never really understanding the details, only knowing that their parents or relatives participated in them. Modern day tandas can go very bad very quickly if one person cheats, takes off with the money, or quits paying after receiving their compensation, leaving the tanda high and dry.

Worrying about getting ripped off may be distracting for the employee, but what if instead of a tanda, the employee falls prey to the sympathies and resources of a union? As discussed in a later chapter in this book, unions are also in a unique position to assist employees like Maria. Unions could easily poach your workforce with the promise of union benefits, and worse, cause major upheaval. Unions dangle "free" immigration law information sessions and attorney consultations to potential members to entice them to join their ranks, but an employee who has enough cash on hand to handle their immigration issues themselves will not be enticed by unions' offers of "free" assistance.

Having a company loan policy in place is necessary to protect both you and your employees. Your policy will set standards on the maximum amount of money you will loan, the payment terms, and justifications for a loan.

WHAT'S IN THE POLICY

A uniform, non-discriminatory employee lending policy can protect your company legally and can provide a useful framework for handling employees' requests for loans. The policy might include statements saying (1) the company has the right to offer loans on a case-by-case basis, (2) loans are based on how long the employee has been with the company, and (3) employees agree to have loan repayments deducted from their wages. The policy could include (4) specific criteria or circumstances under which loans may be offered, as well as (5) the process for evaluating the request. We also recommend that employers include a standard clause stating that (6) employees are responsible to pay even in the event of termination.

We cannot emphasize enough the importance of having a policy in place and enforcing it consistently. Completely independent of immigration concerns, in some circumstances business owners could be sued under discrimination laws if they give out loans to some workers but not others based simply on the whim of the employer.

Get It in Writing. Always document the terms of a loan. Legal documents you may need to include a promissory note stating the terms of the loan and a separate acknowledgement form that states that the employee authorizes the employer to deduct a specified repayment amount from his or her paycheck each week.

Check Laws. If you're deducting loan payments from an employee's paycheck, make sure you aren't violating state wage laws. In some states, it is illegal to pay an employee less than minimum wage after you've taken the loan repayment deduction from their paycheck. Additionally, in some states, if an employee quits before the loan is paid, it may be illegal to deduct the loan balance from the employee's final paycheck.

Stay Honest in Bookkeeping. To avoid trouble with the IRS, make sure you're really offering the employee a loan and not a payment that you don't expect the employee to repay. Loans are not taxed and it is illegal to disguise wages or bonuses as loans for tax purposes. Be diligent and honest in keeping records.

Evaluating the Request. Perhaps the toughest part of establishing a policy is being consistent in how you evaluate requests, especially where you have a close relationship with an individual employee. Some businesses condition a loan on whether or not the employee's performance merits a loan. In other cases, the employer may condition a loan on whether it supports a worthy cause, and not just an employee's bad spending habits.

A worthy cause may be to lend to employees who are experiencing a hardship such as the inability to purchase food or pay rent. However, under the current immigration law, instead of asking what the loan is for, it may also be appropriate to avoid a difficult conversation and an unfortunate outcome, as illustrated in Maria's case, and simply ask only for affirmation that the loan is not being used frivolously. Alternately, your policy may be to place a limit on the amount you are willing to loan for an unspecified event.

Setting the Amount. If you are a small business owner thinking about giving loans to your employees, first and foremost, lend only an amount you can afford to lose. Some employees may consistently face financial troubles and keep coming back to you to ask for help. We advise employers to set an annual cap on the amount of money that an employee can borrow to avoid being inundated with requests that they are not prepared to meet.

On the flip side, employers should consider that a tax-free, interest-free $1000 loan granted in an emergency might be more appreciated by an employee than a taxable $5,000 pay raise apportioned over the course of a year.

CHAPTER 5
NOTARIO FRAUD AND OTHER SCAMS TARGETING HISPANIC LABORERS

"The immigrant culture has an understandable tendency to trust in the ways of their respective countries of origin."

Meet Julian. He knows firsthand what it is like to be conned. Unable to get consistent work because he lacked a Social Security number and had a physical disability, he earned barely enough to cover his rent, much less to feed and clothe his four children.

In desperation Julian sought the help of someone working in a seemingly legitimate business storefront near his local grocery and claiming to be an "immigration specialist" who used to work for U.S. Customs and Immigration Service (USCIS). The man was pleasant, seemingly sincere and appeared knowledgeable. He told Julian it would probably take two years, but he "guaranteed" Julian that he could get him the work authorization papers he needed. Julian was quoted a price of $5,000.

Julian paid a deposit of $1,500, followed by another payment of $90. Soon he was making monthly payments in increments of $100 to $250.

Now, after five years, the only papers he holds in his hands are the stack of documents the immigration specialist claimed to have filed on his behalf—but never did, Julian has since learned from immigration authorities. Today, he does not have work authorization, and his chance of ever obtaining permanent residency in the United States has been jeopardized.

A NOTARIO IS NOT AN ATTORNEY IN THE UNITED STATES

In many Latin American countries a notario is the equivalent of an abogado, or attorney. In others, the title denotes someone who is a public official with quasi-judicial power. However, in the United States, a notario, or notary, is simply someone legally empowered to witness and certify documents and take affidavits. They are not licensed to practice law.

Yet in most heavily Latino U.S. communities, notarios knowingly advertise themselves as accepted practitioners of law. Even worse, notarios prey on the tendency of the immigrant culture to trust in the ways of their country of origin. Unfortunately, enumerable immigration scams exploiting the Spanish word "notario" have bilked thousands of immigrants out of millions of dollars while purporting to legalize their United States residency.

THE IMPORTANCE OF WARNING EMPLOYEES ABOUT NOTARIO FRAUD

In cities and towns across the U.S., notarios advertise their status as "immigration consultants."

You have probably seen the advertisements. On billboards, on buses, and in Spanish-language newspapers, notarios represent themselves to their cultural community as someone who can legally assist with immigration problems. This of course is not accurate and has proven to be highly damaging to many immigrants seeking assistance with their documentation.

There are several organizations committed to ending notario fraud and warning the community about the dangers of using notarios. Both the USCIS and the American Immigration Lawyers Association (AILA) offer free downloadable brochures, signs, and posters for employers who want to warn their employees about notarios. They also provide phone numbers to report notario fraud.

Often, the victims of notario fraud are unaware that they can permanently lose opportunities to pursue actual immigration relief because a notario has damaged their case.

For example, notarios tell Mexican immigrants that being granted asylum can greatly improve the possibility of being awarded a work permit while their immigration case is pending adjudication, and Mexican immigrants may naively sign applications for asylum. But the truth is that successful political asylum applications for Mexican nationals are rare. When the individual is finally called up for an asylum interview, their case is usually revealed as being invalid—and, in many instances, can actually damage any later legitimate case for actual relief from deportation.

Notario scams often spell disaster for immigrants desperate for a shot at permanent residency in the United States. The immigrants not only lose their money but also often face deportation or remain in limbo after many years of struggle. Further, notario fraud bodes ill for you, the employer. It is likely to put tremendous financial and emotional strain on your employee, enough to impact productivity and loss of focus. And, should things go bad and an individual's status be exposed, you could even lose a good worker.

STILL, THE FRAUD THRIVES

Miriam ran an immigration scheme out of her apartment. By the time she was caught by authorities she had defrauded 38 people out of an estimated $250,000. She worked her scam by telling clients that while changes to immigration status can often take several years, she had the political connections to speed up their requests.

Employers have a vested interest in warning their workforce against hiring notarios because it could permanently impact the worker's immigration status.

One day, Miriam met Rodrigo, a 26-year-old taxi driver, when she was a passenger in his cab. She started a conversation by asking him if he had a driver's license. She then immediately began to promise him help in obtaining all kinds of documents, legally. He fell for her pitch. Rodrigo ended up giving her all the money he earned in nine months of work.

After he paid an initial fee of $5000, she told him he needed to bring other people into the arrangement because she could process the applications only in groups of ten. So, he invited relatives and friends, who provided Miriam copies of their tax returns, passports, credit card and bank statements, birth certificates, and even family photographs.

To build their trust, Miriam told each client that she had scheduled them an appointment with immigration authorities, but the appointments turned out to be false, according to officials and court documents.

Sadly for Rodrigo, though Miriam's fraud was ultimately exposed, he lost his savings and exposed himself to further legal problems.

WHAT YOU CAN DO

Perhaps the best thing an employer can do for his or her employees is to inform them of the facts and warn them of the consequences. Explain to your immigrant workforce that notarios are not attorneys in the U.S. even though they may work in a lawyer's office or through a legal referral service. While notarios may appear legitimate, they are not licensed to practice law, and they cannot represent people before immigration authorities.

"ATTORNEYS, ADVOCATES TO IMMIGRANTS: BEWARE OF NOTARIO FRAUD" By AJ Vicens, Tuscon Sentinel, (April 12, 2013)

Spanish-speaking immigrants working their way through the federal immigration system often seek legal services from notarios, people who pose as attorneys while charging much less than lawyers.

Too often, immigration attorneys and advocates say, notarios take money from desperate people and cause major problems in their immigration cases. They say the problem will only get worse with people applying for the Obama administration's deferred action program and anticipating immigration reform.

"Any time there is the idea of new amnesty or reform, we see (notarios) coming out of the woodwork, we see offices popping up out of nowhere," said Fernando Quiroz, executive director of American Beginnings, an immigration advocacy group in Yuma.

Maria Elena-Upson, spokeswoman for U.S. Citizenship and Immigration Services, said the agency has investigated six claims of notario fraud in Arizona during the past year. The numbers are likely much higher, she said, because those in the U.S. illegally are reluctant to file official reports. In Yuma, Quiroz said he's worked with families who were afraid to report notario fraud.

...the [Arizona] State Bar has the authority to investigate and pursue anybody acting like an attorney, but it needs cases to investigate first.

Here are some facts and strategies that you will want your employees to know and understand:

A Law Degree Is Not a License to Practice Law. Notarios may produce a diploma of a law degree from another country to make people believe that they are "official." But a law degree from another country does not qualify as a license to practice law in the U.S. While any person with a law degree may apply for admission to a U.S. state bar, it involves passing a stringent written test (passing the bar), as well as meeting other criteria in order to receive a license to practice law in the U.S.

Be Suspicious. Emphasize to your employees that they should be very suspicious of a notario that says his or her work is "100 percent guaranteed." It is an immediate tip-off that someone is not a legitimate attorney. Licensed attorneys in the U.S. are never allowed to guarantee results. It is an ethics violation and could cause an attorney to lose their license to practice law altogether.

Make it very clear to your employees that a notario may promise or say anything he or she wants to say because there is no oversight for their profession or governing board that hears client complaints. Should they discover that they are being ripped off, there is no recourse. Conversely, a licensed attorney is subject to a governing board that is charged with ensuring attorneys perform within a myriad of ethics

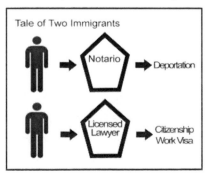

Tale of Two Immigrants

Notario → Deportation

Licensed Lawyer → Citizenship Work Visa

rules regarding professional standards, including how they may or may not advertise their services and communicate with clients.

Confidentiality is Essential. A licensed attorney is always the best option when choosing immigration assistance because attorneys are required by law to keep all conversations completely confidential. We have heard of many cases where a notario uses exposure of confidential information as blackmail to keep the immigrant client paying.

Provide a List of Qualified Lawyers. Some employers may choose to vet local attorneys and provide to employees the names and contact information of those that are licensed and qualified to practice immigration law. In addition, you may even consider offering a free lunch-break seminar hosted by a local attorney to share information about paths to citizenship and how to avoid mistakes. In many urban areas, nonprofit legal clinics affiliated with local law schools can help your employees with immigration status issues.

Notario fraud is not limited to small-time operators working from their apartments or cheap storefronts. You will find them in numerous immigrant-assistance organizations and federations, travel agencies, English-language schools, tax preparers, and even churches. In exchange for your employees' hard-earned dollars—and perhaps those acquired through a company loan—notarios will gladly file incorrect papers and use unaccredited lawyers to do absolutely nothing to advance their case, and may in fact get your employee deported.

Experts say the increase in unlicensed notarios is a byproduct of immigration talk. Every swell in national conversation brings a new wave of fraud. On March 29, 2013, *The Oregonian* reported:

> "As government leaders nationwide gear up for potential immigration reform, officials in Oregon are preparing to combat unlicensed 'notarios': people who pose as tax preparers or lawyers and prey on immigrants.

> "Experts say the increase in unlicensed notarios is a byproduct of immigration talk. Every swell in national conversation brings a new wave of fraud.

> "Oregon regulators recently cracked down on two notarios. Aracely Hernandez of Hillsboro was preparing returns without a license and giving immigration advice without a law degree. Tirsa G. Fong-Guien of Medford was preparing returns filled with errors. Both women were targeting members of the Latino and immigrant communities."

The article goes on to detail the plight of a local nursery worker, who personally knows the extent to which fraudulent notarios can harm unsuspecting immigrants. The worker had been in the U.S. since 1989 without documentation. He met Hernandez in 2008 through a friend when he paid her $500 to do his taxes. He entrusted her with his driver's license, birth certificate, Mexican consular identification and the original documents of his wife, children and grandchildren.

> "She never gave him a receipt. Still, he expected good work based on his friend's positive recommendation.

Avoid Immigration Scams Educational Tools: Posters and information from the Unauthorized Practice of Immigration Law Initiative can be found at www.uscis.gov.

"What the man didn't expect: No tax return, a five-year battle for the documents he still hasn't gotten back, and a string of threats from Hernandez if he spoke out about the issue.

"'She threatened me, saying she was going to call immigration,' he said. 'I was scared. She is also Latina and knows how hard we work. That's what I don't understand about her. No one deserves to be treated like that. It is bad for the community because, really, she was swindling people.'"

In February 2013, the Oregon State Board of Tax Practitioners investigated Hernandez after he and several other people accused her of taking money without completing returns, refusing to return documents and threatening clients who complained. By filing a complaint, the man ultimately helped put Hernandez out of business.

CHAPTER 6
UNIONS, IMMIGRATION REFORM, AND YOU

"When a car wash in Los Angeles unionized, its workers saw benefits improve. One worker saw his weekly pay double and he was able to move into a bigger apartment."

Immigrants without work authorization often accept being underpaid. They are vulnerable because they fear deportation. For them, the promise of higher wages and more benefits through union membership—coupled with a sense of organizational legitimization and representation—holds incredible appeal and may be difficult to refuse. Unions are keenly aware of this appeal and work to exploit it.

Consider the city of Los Angeles. Los Angeles has approximately 500 car washes that employ roughly 10,000 workers, most of them Latinos believed to be unlawfully in the United States. According to a February 14, 2013, Wall Street Journal article, three of those car washes had recently signed union contracts, making employees members of the local United Steelworkers union. As a result, workers saw their weekly pay double. Those workers also got breaks, free drinking water and working gear.

The Service Employees International Union (SEIU) attracts and organizes immigrants in cities with large Hispanic workforces such as Houston and Los Angeles with promises of wage increases, paid personal days, and vacation. About one-fourth of SEIU's 2.1 million members are Hispanic, including many Latin American immigrants who work as janitors, security guards, or healthcare aides. Most members are assumed to be legal residents or U.S. citizens, but unions do not ask workers about their immigration status as a condition to membership. While unions are an issue for employers now, when immigration reform passes and more immigrants hold work authorization, employers can expect that more workers—emboldened by their new legal status and secured with documentation—will soften to the calls of unions.

The upcoming changes in immigration reform are creating a confusing environment for immigrants. They are inundated with questions and are scared to ask for the answers. Employers are in a unique position to assist immigrants, and the ways in which employers inform and assist them during this time is pivotal in keeping businesses union-free and flexible in the marketplace.

THE CHANGING LANDSCAPE OF UNION TACTICS

Because unions have seen how deep the immigrant labor pool runs and how accepting immigrant workers increases membership dues and collective bargaining power, unions have done a complete turn-around in recent years regarding their stance on immigration reform and their attitude toward immigrant laborers.

Historically, the American Federation of Labor (AFL) has had a very negative approach toward immigrant labor because immigrants accept lower wages, are able to break strikes and reduce the unions' collective-bargaining power. Additionally, many AFL arguments were eugenics-based, considering Southern and Eastern Europeans, Asians, and Latinos as "inferior races." Even National Farm Workers Association founder Cesar Chavez, who history has canonized as a compassionate advocate for immigrant workers, was in fact vehemently opposed to illegal immigration. In 1969, Chavez led a march from the Coachella and Imperial Valleys of California to Mexico to protest the use of illegal aliens as strikebreakers. But of course, towards the end of the 20th century, as the United States labor force became increasingly diverse, many unions were forced to shift their position on immigrant labor or risk losing money and power.

The percentage of unionized U.S. workers—11.3 percent—is roughly half what it was 30 years ago. Perhaps more important to note is that from 2002 to 2012 Latino union membership increased by 21 percent, while Caucasian membership was reduced by close to 13 percent, according to the Labor Department's Bureau of Labor Statistics. Today, union leaders see immigrant workers—particularly newly documented ones who are more likely to join—as a bright star that could safeguard unions' futures amid public-sector budget constraints and a trend toward weakening collective-bargaining rights.

To unions, immigrant workers who are trying to gain status represent a major class of potential dues-paying members. In this context, passing immigration legislation is a top priority for labor unions. Believing that organizing immigrant workers can swell unions' shrinking ranks, unions are spending millions of dollars on advertising, rallies and letter-writing campaigns to lawmakers to push their immigration agenda.

Further, unions are throwing political muscle behind lawmakers' efforts to overhaul immigration regulations. Two of the most important labor unions in the county, the AFL-CIO and Change to Win, have endorsed President Obama's plan for comprehensive immigration reform. And early in 2013, AFL-CIO President Richard Trumka, other labor leaders and executives from companies such as Coca-Cola Co. and Goldman Sachs Group Inc. met with President Obama to discuss their interests.

Labor unions argue that in order to ensure all workers' rights are protected across the board, the playing field must be level so that undocumented workers do not receive disparate treatment or suffer abuse because of their undocumented status. To that end, unions advise that a level playing field can only be created if undocumented immigrant workers become union members so that they are under the blanket of the unions' protection. Unions tell immigrants that only with legalized status can unions protect labor standards for all workers.

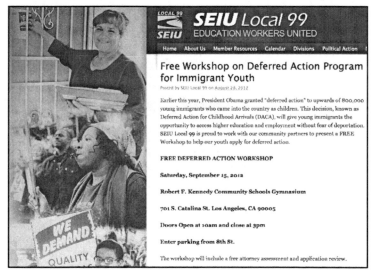

In addition to making immigrant workers believe that only unions can protect labor standards, unions employ many tactics to recruit immigrant workers to become members. One tactic labor unions use to induce immigrant workers to join their ranks is to host free workshops and information sessions on issues paramount to immigrant workers. A quick glance at Teamsters Local Union No. 890's Facebook page demonstrates how frequently such workshops and information sessions are held.

Common union tactics include:

- Promise of permanent residency
- General membership perks
- Free immigration consultations
- Free review of application
- Discounted legal services
- Bilingual immigration rights kit

UNIONS OFFER EDUCATION

More and more, unions are offering workshops for Hispanic member prospects. These include DACA workshops offered by the SEIU Local 99, which include "a free attorney assessment and application review" for all attendees. Note that these workshops are not entirely "free," as they require immigrant workers to present proof that they have attended a union information session in order to receive the immigration information. On the SEIU Local 99 website, they advise potential workshop attendees that "anyone wishing to participate in the workshop must have attended an information session and come prepared with the necessary supporting documents."

Unions operate under a guise of protection for all laborers, but their real objective is increased membership. Often, employees can't decipher unions' objectives. Employees in need of immigration assistance may be especially blinded by their own need for the unions' offers of immigration help. Keep in mind that an employee with enough cash on hand—perhaps thanks to a company loan as discussed in Chapter 4—can be immune to unions' tactic of increasing membership by providing "free" legal assistance in immigration matters.

In light of the unions' interests and the resources being deployed to push immigration reform, employers have an obvious and vested interest in keeping their immigrant workforce from attending union fairs and seminars. Unions advertise complete immigration assistance for members—and do not doubt that it is a huge calling card. To counteract this tactic, we strongly recommend that employers match union offers, if possible, and help employees attain legal services through them.

TIPS FOR FAIR LABOR PRACTICES

- Threaten: Never threaten to retaliate against employees with termination or reducing pay or benefits.
- Interrogate: Never interrogate employees about their activites or activies of co-workers (including social media activities)
- Promise: Do not promise promotions or benefits in exchange for their promise not support the union.
- Spy: Never spy on union activities as employees have a legal right to meet with union representatives and "hear them out" without management interference.

CAUTION: Take special heed to note that if employees have already begun organizing into a union, employers must follow federal laws on elections. Once union organization commences, the law strictly regulates what employers can and cannot say and do. You cannot spy, threaten, question, or promise any kind of benefit to employees for voting down the union. If you do, you can be sanctioned with unfair labor practices.

The acronym **TIPS** can help you to remember what you must refrain from doing: **Do not threaten, interrogate, promise, or spy.**

The minute you believe that your employees are becoming softened by union tactics or are considering organization, immediately consult your attorney.

KEEPING YOUR WORKPLACE UNION-FREE

Almost all places of employment are eligible for union organization—there is no minimum size or type of industry required for a union to represent employees. However, there are strategies employers can use to minimize the likelihood that employees would accept the formation of a union.

"LABOR UNIONS HAVE A BIG STAKE IN IMMIGRATION REFORM" By Adrian Florido, *KPBS*, San Diego, (April 10, 2013)

Union membership has been declining steadily for decades. Legalizing the 11 million immigrants without current legal status could be a boon for union membership and their ability to raise wages and living standards.

"For 11 million workers to know that the boss is not going to be able to intimidate them because of their immigration status," [Maria Elena] Durazo [one of the U.S.'s most powerful union leaders] said. "It's going to bring them out of the shadows give them a lot more confidence and courage to stand up for their rights."

This at least partly explains the shift that organized labor has made in its position toward immigrant and guest workers. For decades, labor unions had a tense relationship with workers who were in the country illegally. They're hard to organize and easy to exploit, which unions see as driving wages down for all workers.

Employers may think that increased pay and benefits are the only reasons employees are influenced to join a union, but according to research conducted by the Society for Human Resource Management, employees also join unions because they are dissatisfied with their treatment and believe that a union can make workplace conditions better. It is the total package presented by unions that lures employees into buying into unions' perceived ills—that the company is unfair, unresponsive, or offering substandard working conditions.

Employers looking to minimize employee dissatisfaction can also minimize employees' desire for union representation by employing your own strategies.

- Establish fair and consistent policies and practices.
- Maintain open-door management policies. Communication is vital!
- Offer competitive pay and benefits.
- Foster employee trust and recognition. Acknowledge and value good work.
- Facilitate the path to finding immigration services. Provide employees with a list of attorneys and host seminars explaining new immigration laws.

A workplace that fosters good relationships between management and employees and that promptly and consistently addresses employees' concerns is less likely to drive employees to union representation for assistance. If you are doing your job as an employer by posting informative Department of Labor bulletins, apprising your workforce of immigration reform updates, maintaining good working conditions, and in some situations perhaps issuing company loans, then your employees will have no need for a union in the first place.

Chapter 7
DON'T GET ICED: I-9 WORKPLACE INSPECTIONS ARE TARGETING EMPLOYERS

"Worksite enforcement and immigration related employment fines continue to be at the forefront of U.S. Immigration and Customs Enforcement priorities."

Like the rest of the country, Monty & Ramirez LLP is excited about immigration reform. However, employers must understand that immigration reform has not happened yet and the order of the day is still compliance with existing law. Do not let the hype of immigration reform lull you into believing that compliance should be ignored or forgotten. In fact, the immigration reform proposals currently on the table all call for more compliance. And that includes the release of a new Employee Eligibility Verification Form, or the Form I-9. Further, two bills were introduced by Congress in early 2013 "to make the E-Verify Program mandatory and expand the use of E-Verify."

Today's Hispanic workplace and workforce face increased pressures regarding employment authorizations and verifications, calling for heightened awareness by employers and managers. With political and public sentiment at an all-time high regarding how immigrant workers should factor into America's labor workforce, it is imperative that employers continue to be diligent in complying with current employment laws. Among the more common missteps employers with large immigrant workforces make are improper preparation, verification and handling of the I-9.

And employer audits are a growing part of the Obama administration's immigration enforcement strategy. Under George W. Bush, U.S. Immigration & Customs Enforcement (ICE) employed frequent workplace raids and arrested undocumented immigrants on the job, but the Obama administration, on the other hand, believes targeting employers is a more effective and humane approach. Company investigations are one of the pillars of President Obama's immigration policy, focusing agency resources on the investigation and audit of employers suspected of cultivating illegal workplaces by hiring workers who are not authorized to work.

Table 4. Criminal Indictments and Convictions Related to Worksite Enforcement Investigations, FY2005-FY2011		
Fiscal Year	Indictments	Convictions
2005	254	156
2006	411	340
2007	750	561
2008	900	908
2009	361	339
2010	404	333
2011	639	586

Source: CRS presentation of data from U.S. Department of Homeland Security, Immigration and Customs Enforcement, July 1, 2008 (FY2005-FY2007), April 22, 2010 (FY2008-FY2009), February 10, 2011 (FY2010), and April 27, 2012 (FY2011).

Note: A conviction may occur in the same year as the related indictment or in a subsequent year.

In fiscal year 2012, ICE made 520 criminal arrests tied to worksite enforcement investigations. Of the individuals criminally arrested, 240 were owners, managers, supervisors, or human resources employees. Charges include harboring or knowingly hiring illegal aliens. The remaining workers who were criminally arrested face charges such as aggravated identity theft and Social Security fraud. In 2012, ICE also debarred 376 business and individuals for administrative and criminal violations and served a record-breaking 3,004 Notices of Inspection (NOI) on companies. ICE monetary fines have grown from $1 million in 2009 to $13 million in 2012.

Now more than ever is the time for employers to revise their compliance procedures to include new policies concerning the proper completion, retention and auditing of I-9s. Do not wait until ICE issues your business a NOI to make the necessary corrections; it could be too late. Civil and criminal penalties issued by ICE can place a business in bankruptcy and owners and supervisors in prison. Take preventive measures now and contact a law firm that specializes in Form I-9 compliance to conduct an external audit of your business today. Your company will only have a 72-hour window to produce current and terminated employee I-9s from the time an NOI is issued. In the event that your company is investigated, you should **immediately** retain an attorney in order to mitigate civil and criminal penalties.

During an ICE investigation, investigators routinely subpoena records of all current employees, as well as any employees terminated within the last three years. The three-year period relates to the record-keeping requirement for former employees, which is three years from the date of hire or one year from the date of termination, whichever date is later in time. In addition, investigators will require that the employer produce a roster of and supporting documentation for all independent contractors, temporary staff from an agency and "on-call" individuals, which are then dutifully scrutinized.

Beyond I-9s, during an ICE investigation the employer will be required to produce payroll reports, quarterly tax statements with the IRS, state unemployment insurance tax reports, and other corporate information such as articles of incorporation, employer identification number, owner's social security number, business license, and annual reports. Investigators will also consider whether the company is a current or previous E-Verify member. ICE will use this information to assess the company's compliance.

The remainder of this chapter provides insight into the relevant changes made to the new Form I-9, steps employers must take to comply going forward and information employers should know about the consequences of failing to comply with U.S. employment and immigration law.

I-9 NEWS

One need only glance at the headlines to know that work-site enforcement by the federal government is increasing in the government's stated attempt to reduce the demand for illegal employment and to protect employment opportunities for the nation's lawful workforce. In the past year, ICE and Homeland Security Investigations (HSI) have emphasized increased utilization of all available civil and administrative tools, including Form I-9 inspections, civil fines and debarment from government contracts in efforts to strengthen the integrity of the U.S. workforce and to curtail the employment of unauthorized workers.

No company large or small is immune. In recent years, ICE auditors hit ethnic stores, restaurants, bakeries, manufacturing companies, construction companies, food packaging operations, janitorial services, catering businesses, dairies, and farms. Among some of the largest businesses hit with an NOI in 2012 was Atrium. Atrium, the owner of Houston-based Champion Window, is the largest manufacturer and distributor of residential vinyl and aluminum windows and patio doors in the United States with a total workforce around 3,700 employees.

Atrium agreed to forfeit $2 million for falsely attesting on I-9 forms that work authorization documents presented by new hires appeared genuine. The ICE investigation also revealed that 269 of Champion's 451-person workforce consisted of undocumented aliens. A follow-up investigation revealed that 8.3 percent of parent company Atrium's 3,382 employees were also undocumented workers. This case study illustrates how a subsidiary company's I-9 errors can lead ICE to issue a follow up investigation on the parent company's I-9s and result in heavy fines.

PENALTIES FOR PROHIBITED PRACTICES

If your business fails to properly complete, retain, and/or make available for inspection Forms I-9, your company may face monetary penalties of $110 to $1,100 per I-9 for "paper" violations. If you are convicted of having engaged in the practice of knowingly hiring unauthorized aliens, fines may accrue up to $3,000 per employee and/or six months imprisonment. The maximum penalty for harboring illegal aliens is five years in prison and a $250,000 fine for each count.

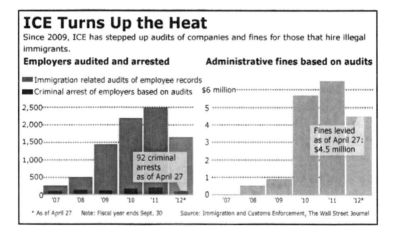

ICE Turns Up the Heat

Since 2009, ICE has stepped up audits of companies and fines for those that hire illegal immigrants.

Employers audited and arrested

Administrative fines based on audits

CRIMINAL ARRESTS CONTINUE

Patterns uncovered in an I-9 audit that suggest technical errors were not simply inadvertent but an attempt, for example, to disguise illegal employment practices, harbor undocumented workers or practice reverse discrimination, company owners, managers and human resource professionals can be held criminally liable.

Lately, ICE has emphasized its criminal investigations of managers. For example, a Dunkin' Donuts manager in Maine was sentenced to home arrest for knowingly hiring undocumented immigrants, and a manager of an Illinois staffing firm got 18 months in prison.

In June 2011, Homeland Security Investigations (DHS) special agents and the Williamsport (Pennsylvania) Bureau of Police officers arrested 19 aliens employed by GPX, a Texas seismic surveying company, at apartments rented for them by GPX. On March 12, 2013, GPX plead guilty to harboring and transporting illegal aliens and agreed to forfeit $250,000 cash and pay a $25,000 fine. The investigation revealed that GPX and its field operations supervisor, Douglas Wiggill, hired the 19 illegal aliens to work on a seismic surveying project in Lycoming County, Pennsylvania. The federal indictment alleged that GPX failed to verify the immigration status of the aliens and did not prepare the required Forms I-9 and supporting documentation concerning the aliens' authorization to be in the United States. Wiggill pleaded guilty to a misdemeanor charge of aiding the improper entry of aliens into the U.S. He faces six months in prison and a $5,000 fine.

BEST PRACTICES TO PROTECT YOUR COMPANY NOW!

Designate One Qualified Individual to Manage and Keep Form I-9s. No matter how large or small your management staff or how far and widespread your operations, a wise strategy is to designate one individual to handle all I-9s. You will find that this one step makes the task more manageable, helps to avoid missteps and makes furnishing records easier should the government come calling.

For example, an employee's Form I-9 must be kept separate from their personnel files. Assigning a designated individual to handle I-9s, one who does not also handle routine employee personnel files, benefits plans or other workplace issues, will make compliance easy. Further, because the Form I-9 must be available at the workplace for inspection by authorized U.S. government officials from the DHS, Department of Labor, or Department of Justice—who may drop in with only three days notice—the designated individual can avoid unnecessary delay in producing the documents and possibly eliminate further inspection or questioning.

A Designated I-9 Expert Ensures Compliance. As mentioned above, the fines for failing to properly complete the Form I-9 can be quite hefty. The individual designated for I-9 compliance across the enterprise will serve as the gatekeeper for form completeness and accuracy. For example, this individual will be tasked with ensuring that an "authorized individual" is signing the attestation in Section 2 to verify authenticity of documents produced to prove work authorization. They will crosscheck documentation numbers and keep track of employee work-authorization expiration dates. They will manage record storage and be responsible for monitoring and destroying the forms of retired or terminated employees—a task that can easily fall by the wayside if not charged to a specific, conscientious individual.

And finally, he or she will be charged with keeping up-to-date on United States Citizenship and Immigration Services (USCIS), DHS, Form I-9, and E-Verify changes. They will be your point guard responsible to communicate changes to hiring managers, personnel staff, and others that need to know.

Establish an Internal I-9 Training Program. As we now recognize, ICE agents scrutinize I-9s. If they notice non-compliance or a pattern of identity fraud, they will expand their search to other facilities or more frequently today, go companywide. Therefore, employers should make sure that all their human resource staff and hiring managers are very familiar with the I-9 process. At the very least the company should mandate reading and digesting the M-274 Handbook for Employers (available for download from www.uscis.gov). However, reading materials are rarely enough. Employers should consider providing onsite seminars, training workshops, access to online classes, and a direct line to legal counsel who is intimately familiar with I-9 compliance and related issues and can answer any unusual questions should they arise in the course of business.

The I-9 Audit Saves Time, Money and Headaches. When it comes to I-9s, E-Verify and worksite compliance, employers need to be proactive and preemptive. Now, with the new I-9 form in place, is a great time to conduct an internal I-9 audit of all employee records.

Whether you use in-house legal counsel or a knowledgeable employment or immigration law attorney to conduct the audit, a careful review of existing I-9s is going to be your best defense. An I-9 audit can help your company avoid significant fines, negative publicity, and even criminal charges.

Establish a Written I-9 Compliance Policy. A clearly written—in plain English—compliance policy for all managers and resource personnel will not only increase quality assurance, but it is a solid preemptive risk-management strategy. As noted above in the section on ICE investigations, having a policy and procedure in place is a sign to investigators that you are making a good-faith attempt to comply with the rules. Another sign of good faith is the government's E-verify program, which we expect to be a mandatory requirement of immigration reform, based on the Gang of Eight's proposal.

In the year 2013, or as soon as possible, is a perfect time to institute a policy that includes changes as a result of the new Form I-9. The policy should include what is and isn't expected of hiring managers and human resource professionals, and any explanation regarding consequences for non-compliance. Provide a copy of the new (or revised) policy to each and every employee charged with processing and managing the I-9 function at your company. Remember also to provide live support for answering questions or a brief training session to ensure that all those that need to know are aware of the changes and are equipped to properly implement them. Do not guess. Consult a trusted professional in the field to help you or to guide you when questions or challenges arise.

WHAT'S NEW ABOUT THE NEW FORM I-9?

On March 8, 2013, the USCIS released an improved Form I-9. The revised form has several new features, including a new two-page format, a clearer description of the information employees and employers must provide in each section, and new data fields for an email address, phone number, "other" name, and foreign passport number. The instruction sheet is now six pages.

When to Use It. Employers should begin using the new Form I-9 with the revision date of 03/08/13 immediately for all new hires, as well as for rehires or re-verifications. Beginning May 7, 2013, employers must only use the new Form I-9.

HIGHLIGHTS AND EXPLANATION OF THE I-9 FORM CHANGES
Section 1 (Employer Review and Attestation)

Section 1. Employee Information and Attestation *(Employees must complete and sign Section 1 of Form I-9 no later than the first day of employment, but not before accepting a job offer.)*

Last Name *(Family Name)*	First Name *(Given Name)*	Middle Initial	Other Names Used *(if any)*
Doe	John	A	N/A

Address *(Street Number and Name)*	Apt. Number	City or Town	State	Zip Code
123 Main Street	1	Washington	DC	20000

Date of Birth *(mm/dd/yyyy)*	U.S. Social Security Number	E-mail Address	Telephone Number
01/01/1960	0 0 0 - 0 0 - 0 0 0 0	johndoe@email.com	(202) 123-4567

I am aware that federal law provides for imprisonment and/or fines for false statements or use of false documents in connection with the completion of this form.

I attest, under penalty of perjury, that I am (check one of the following):

☐ A citizen of the United States

☐ A noncitizen national of the United States *(See instructions)*

☐ A lawful permanent resident (Alien Registration Number/USCIS Number): _____

☒ An alien authorized to work until (expiration date, if applicable, mm/dd/yyyy) 02/28/2015 Some aliens may write "N/A" in this field. *(See instructions)*

For aliens authorized to work, provide your Alien Registration Number/USCIS Number OR Form I-94 Admission Number:

1. Alien Registration Number/USCIS Number: 1 2 3 4 5 6 7 8 9

OR

2. Form I-94 Admission Number: _____

> 3-D Barcode
> Do Not Write in This Space

If you obtained your admission number from CBP in connection with your arrival in the United States, include the following:

Foreign Passport Number: _____

Country of Issuance: _____

Some aliens may write "N/A" on the Foreign Passport Number and Country of Issuance fields. *(See instructions)*

Signature of Employee	*John A. Doe*	Date *(mm/dd/yyyy)*	Date Employee Completes Section 1

Maiden Name is now called "Other Names Used (if any)." Per the instructions, "Provide all other names used, if any (including your maiden name). Write N/A if you've not had other legal names."

The Social Security Number (SSN) boxes are now formatted to fit the requisite 9 digits.

Email Address and Telephone Number are new fields. Completing these fields is voluntary for the employee, but are not marked as such on the form itself. However, if the employee volunteers this information, ICE may use it to contact your employee directly if DHS learns of a potential mismatch between the information provided and the information in DHS or Social Security Administration (SSA) records.

A-Number vs. USCIS Number. The instructions note that the "USCIS number is the same as the A-number without the "A" prefix." Further clarification states that foreigners authorized to work can provide either the A-Number/USCIS Number OR the Form I-94 number.

Form I-94 Admission Number. The admission number on Form I-94 or "as directed by U.S. Customs and Border Protection in connection with your arrival in the United States" leaves room for future procedural changes.

3-D Barcode. USCIS is developing a "Smart Form I-9" to be completed online, which will list information presented by the employee and create a barcode in the 3-D Barcode space provided on the Form I-9.

Section 2 (Employer Review and Verification)

Section 2. Employer or Authorized Representative Review and Verification

(Employers or their authorized representative must complete and sign Section 2 within 3 business days of the employee's first day of employment. You must physically examine one document from List A OR examine a combination of one document from List B and one document from List C as listed on the "Lists of Acceptable Documents" on the next page of this form. For each document you review, record the following information: document title, issuing authority, document number, and expiration date, if any.)

Employee Last Name, First Name and Middle Initial from Section 1: Doe, John A

List A Identity and Employment Authorization	OR	List B Identity	AND	List C Employment Authorization
Document Title: EAD		Document Title:		Document Title:
Issuing Authority: DHS/USCIS		Issuing Authority:		Issuing Authority:
Document Number: XXX1234567891		Document Number:		Document Number:
Expiration Date (if any)(mm/dd/yyyy): 02/28/2015		Expiration Date (if any)(mm/dd/yyyy):		Expiration Date (if any)(mm/dd/yyyy):
Document Title:				
Issuing Authority:				
Document Number:				
Expiration Date (if any)(mm/dd/yyyy):				3-D Barcode Do Not Write in This Space
Document Title:				
Issuing Authority:				
Document Number:				
Expiration Date (if any)(mm/dd/yyyy):				

Certification

I attest, under penalty of perjury, that (1) I have examined the document(s) presented by the above-named employee, (2) the above-listed document(s) appear to be genuine and to relate to the employee named, and (3) to the best of my knowledge the employee is authorized to work in the United States.

The employee's first day of employment (mm/dd/yyyy): ___See Above___ *(See instructions for exemptions.)*

Signature of Employer or Authorized Representative *Alice Smith*	Date (mm/dd/yyyy) Date Employer Completes Section 2	Title of Employer or Authorized Representative HR Manager		
Last Name (Family Name) Smith	First Name (Given Name) Alice	Employer's Business or Organization Name Widgets, Inc.		
Employer's Business or Organization Address (Street Number and Name) 567 Maple Street	City or Town Washington	State DC	Zip Code 20000	

Section 2 now includes words to make it clearer that an "Authorized Representative," such as designated agent or notary, can act in an agent capacity in completing Section 2.

The new form also requires the employer to list employee's full name at the top of Section 2, in order to identify the record should the Form I-9 pages become separated.

New List A fields have been added to account for student or exchange visitors who present a foreign passport with a Form I-94.

Section 3 (Re-verification and Rehires)

This section received only minor formatting changes.

The List of Acceptable Documents

The attached list contains a clarification of the SSN card restrictions. Although it may seem self-explanatory, it is important to note that if the card has imprinted on it either (1) "Not Valid for Employment," (2) "Valid for Work Only with INS Authorization," or (3) "Valid for Work Only with DNS Authorization," it cannot be used as an acceptable document.

REMEMBER:

1. Hiring employees without complying with the employment eligibility verification requirements of the Form I-9 is against the law, and could result in civil and criminal penalties.
2. Employees hired after November 6, 1986, must present documentation that establishes identity and employment authorization. Employers must record this information on Form I-9.
3. Employers may not discriminate against employees on the basis of national origin or citizenship status.

CHAPTER 8
CONTINUOUS RESIDENCY: ISSUES YOU NEED TO KNOW

Even if employers do all they can to comply with Form I-9 verification, employees may nonetheless produce very legitimate-looking papers that can fool an employer and cause the employer to lose a valuable employee should Immigration and Customs Enforcement (ICE) audit the I-9s. You yourself may not have suspicion that you employ undocumented workers in your workforce and may not find out until a day comes when, for example, a young worker approaches you and says he is undocumented and needs your help proving continuous residency for purposes of DACA.

An employee may have many reasons for soliciting a letter from an employer stating the employee's dates of employment, similar to a service letter. For example, an employee may need such a letter when applying for a mortgage, opening a bank account, or even looking for another job. Still, it is entirely possible that the employee is seeking a service letter for a DACA application in order to prove continuous residency. If the employee reveals to the employer the reason for the request, and DACA is the reason, the employer is put in a very difficult situation.

IS IT OKAY TO PROVIDE A SERVICE LETTER?

According to the U.S. Customs and Immigration Service (USCIS) guidelines, information regarding an applicant's employment dates to support a request under DACA will not be shared with ICE for civil immigration enforcement purposes (Section 274A of the Immigration and Nationality Act) unless there is evidence of egregious violations of criminal statutes or widespread abuses.

An employer who is told that a request for a letter stating employment dates is for DACA application purposes, now has actual knowledge that the employee likely lacks work authorization. Additionally, such actual knowledge may imply constructive knowledge regarding other similarly situated employees who have requested similar letters.

An employer in such a quandary must take corrective action immediately to cure the violation. Termination may be inevitable in order to protect you and your company. But if you are informed and your company has—and consistently follows—a neutral procedure for requesting and issuing service letters, you can avoid complications.

WHAT'S IN THE POLICY

Consider a policy on issuing service letters, but remember NOT to implement it now without understanding the risks that come with actual and constructive knowledge of the immigration status of your workforce.

Regardless, the smart solution is to avoid the hassle altogether by employing a standardized, objective, neutral procedure for issuing service letters. Such a procedure should be set out in a policy.

The service letter issuance policy should include some or all of the following provisions:

(1) The company will provide letters for the actual dates the individual has been employed at the company—without exception.

(2) All requests will contain the employee's or former employee's signature authorizing the release of information.

(3) An authorized officer of the company must sign the letter. You may chose to name the individual or simply state that all requests will be handled through the human resource director or other such company executive.

(4) Exceptions to the policy are rarely made and can only be made if approved by the company's president.

(5) Emphasize that the company will not ask the reason for the request.

(6) State that a request will NOT require a name or address of the person to whom the letter will ultimately be presented because all service letters will be addressed "To whom it may concern." Addressing all letters using "To whom it may Concern" is your best defense against charges of actual or constructive knowledge that you knowingly hired and retained undocumented workers.

If an employee asks his employer for a "reference"—different from a service letter of employment or recommendation—it is best for the employer to simply state the dates the employee worked with the company and not elaborate further. Providing misinformation can cause legal ramifications that may endanger your business.

The crucial point is this: No matter what you choose to include in your policy, you must state it clearly, ensure that it is within the confines of the law, and—as with all employer/employee policies—execute it with consistency.

¡CUIDADO! EMPLOYER/EMPLOYEE COLLUSION CAN HAVE FAR-REACHING EFFECTS

Falsification of documents or records is against the law, period. In the United States the crime is a federal felony and may result in a prison sentence for submitting false documentation to the DHS.

But as Ripley says, "believe it or not," and you can believe it or not, but there are circumstances in which an employer may conciously fail to use good judgment. For example, suppose one of your valuable employees asks for a service letter in order to provide proof of continuous residency in the United States. You know that the employee has not been continuously present in the country, but you are tempted to fabricate the dates of employment in order to assist your employee.

DO NOT DO THIS!

Do not lie about dates—or any other information for that matter—in order to "help" an employee. USCIS and ICE records are digital, and agencies can cross-reference the employment dates you allege with government records. If caught, the legal cost for you will substantially outweigh the benefit of retaining an employee.

Remember, service letters from employers are not required, and there are other ways to prove continuous residency. The employee can prove residency through another means such as utility bills, phone bills, school records, doctor's records, hospital bills, or even receipts of remittances (*remesas* or *envíos*) sent to relatives or friends in their home country over the years. Proving continuous residency does not require employer help. Remember to use great care before deciding to write a service letter.

Some workers, particularly farm workers or others living in temporary or employer-provided housing, may not have other records and thus may truly have difficulty in proving continuous residency without a service letter. Once reform becomes law, employers will have more flexibility in writing service letters. Until then, you must proceed with caution.

Chapter 9
RESPECT THE LAW! ALIENS MUST BEHAVE BETTER THAN CITIZENS OR RISK DEPORTATION

*"Employers that value their immigrant workforce should feel
an implied duty to warn immigrant employees of the consequences that criminal activity can have on their current or
future immigration status. All employers want their workforce to remain free of criminal activity, but this is especially
crucial for immigrant labor. Your immigrant employees are
not likely to be aware of certain laws, and they are even
less likely to be aware of the far-reaching consequences of
breaking them."*

VICTOR'S ENCOUNTER WITH THE LAW—A VERY COMMON STORY

As a child in 1988, Victor escaped to the United States
from El Salvador with his mother. Eight years later he
obtained a green card granting him Lawful Permanent Residency (LPR) status. Then, he impregnated a 13-year-old
fellow student when he was 17, and in 1999 was charged
with aggravated sexual assault of a child—a felony crime.
The girl insisted to authorities that the sex was consensual

and that she had told him she was 16. In fact, the two were married shortly after the birth of their child.

While it may shock our American notion of how kids should behave—children shouldn't have children—it's not necessarily abnormal or uncommon in Central America and Mexico. Despite their marriage, Victor's case was actively prosecuted and in order to avoid jail time, he pled guilty to the offense as charged.

Prior to 1996 a non-citizen had access to the discretion of a judge in criminal cases and would not, by law, be immediately deported upon a conviction. However, since 1996, the law changed and clearly states that a non-citizen, even a LPR (green card holder) convicted of an "aggravated felony"* does not have any relief from deportation.

Without understanding the immigration consequences of his guilty plea, Victor had in fact pled guilty to an aggravated felony, or in other words, he had signed his own deportation order. By mere luck, Victor was not reported to immigration officials, and instead was released and given eight years of probation.

By the time we met Victor, he was in need of an experienced immigration attorney. Victor was in deportation proceedings. Victor learned about the consequences of his plea when he applied for citizenship. By applying for citizenship, he notified immigration officials about his previous conviction.

We took Victor's case pro bono because we believed he and his family were deserving of our help. At this point in

---

* The term "Aggravated Felony," is a term of art defined under Section 101(a)(43) of the Immigration and Nationality Act. It is used to describe a category of offenses that carry very harsh immigration consequences, such as mandatory detention and deportation.

his life, Victor was at the top of his field and had even been a community leader for several years. Yet, despite our best efforts, we could not undo the effects of his previous guilty plea. The immigration judge was not concerned that Victor's prior criminal attorney had no knowledge of immigration law, or that he had convinced Victor to accept a plea, promising that he would just receive probation.

COMPETENT LEGAL HELP

Victor's initial attorney never told him about the immigration consequences of his plea, because he never learned immigration law. Instead, the attorney walked away with $5,000 of Victor's money, and Victor was deported. Victor's criminal case should have gone to trial, but it was easier and faster for the attorney to convince Victor to plead guilty.

Perhaps if Victor had all the facts or had been able to hire a defense attorney that was knowledgeable in immigration law he would be in the U.S. today. If you, the employer, become aware of an immigrant employee being accused or arrested, emphasize to them the importance of speaking with a qualified immigration attorney—immediately. The laws regarding criminal activity and immigration are very complex and one wrong move—such as pleading no-contest on a charge—could cause irrevocable damage to immigration status. It can be a very costly mistake.

An enlightened employer should be able to discuss the consequences of pleas with their immigrant workforce. The employer should also have a list of Spanish-speaking criminal attorneys who are savvy about immigration consequences. The criminal system is intimidating, causing people to rely on their criminal attorneys. The best thing that an employer can do for them when these situations arise is help your employee find good advice from criminal attorneys who are knowledgeable about immigration-safe pleas.

WHAT EMPLOYERS NEED TO KNOW ABOUT IMMIGRANTS AND CRIMINAL CONVICTIONS

As Victor's story illustrates, even if an employee is a Lawful Permanent Resident (LPR), he or she is subject to immediate removal and could be denied any further admission to the United States. If an individual is working illegally and/or has plans to apply for DACA, a criminal conviction before, during, or after the application could disqualify them.

The devil is in the details, as they say. Just because an attorney is licensed to practice law in the United States does not necessarily mean that they are qualified to represent a client in criminal case, let alone a criminal immigration case. For the immigrant, the laws are not simple to understand, nor are they readily available—in foreign language translations. But an employer that takes the time to comprehend the basics and convey the seriousness of a criminal conviction and its effect upon immigration status will be of great help to their immigrant workforce. This one step can impact the success and reliability of their workforce.

A good starting point is to understand that there are differences between how criminal actions impact the LPR and the alien nonimmigrant (NI), which includes guest workers in the U.S. on visas such as the H-1B, L-1 and H-2A.

LAWFUL PERMANENT RESIDENTS

A LPR, sometimes referred to as a "Permanent Resident Alien," "Resident Alien Permit Holder" or "Green Card Holder," may work for your company, enjoy many of the benefits of a U.S. citizen, and can generally travel in and out of the U.S. for reasonable periods of time. If a LPR is eighteen years of age or older, they must carry their valid physical green card at all times. Failing to do so is a violation of the Immigration and Nationality Act, carrying the possibility of a fine up to $100 and/or imprisonment for up to 30 days for each offense.

LPRs do not have the right to vote or to be elected in federal and state elections, however male permanent residents between the ages of 18 and 26 are subject to registering in the Selective Service System, and all LPRs who reside in the United States must pay taxes on their worldwide income, like U.S. citizens.

HOW TO LOSE LAWFUL PERMANENT RESIDENT STATUS

A LPR may be removed from the U.S. because they (1) were inadmissible at the time of entry, (2) violate a condition of their status in the U.S., or (3) commit crimes or other prohibited acts that include, but are not limited to, unlawful voting, false claims of citizenship, document falsification, or failure to notify USCIS of an address change within ten days.

However, a LPR will not typically be regarded as seeking "admission" when returning from foreign travel, and thus not subject to grounds of inadmissibility. Yet, there are exceptions that can jeopardize their status. We recommend that a LPR wishing to leave the U.S. should consult an attorney if they have any doubt.

There are many ways one can lose his or her LPR status.

(1) An individual will typically abandon or relinquish their LPR status if they are continuously absent from the U.S. in excess of 180 days.

(2) A LPR can lose their status if they are engaged in illegal activity after their departure, or depart from the U.S. while in removal or extradition proceedings, or commit a criminal or criminally related offense.*

(3) A LPR cannot be convicted or ADMIT to committing a crime of moral turpitude or a controlled substance violation without jeopardizing resident status. Crimes of violence and those involving baseness, vileness, or depravity or that are defined, to some degree, to violate current moral standards—such as rape, murder, robbery, kidnapping, voluntary manslaughter, theft, spousal abuse, fraud, and aggravated DWI offenses—are considered crimes of moral turpitude. (Note: under DACA even a simple DWI disqualifies an individual.)

(4) If a LPR attempts to enter at a place other than a designated port of entry or have not been admitted

---

* If an LPR commited the crime before 18 years of age and at least five years have passed since the end of any confinement OR if the maximum possible penalty for the crime was less than one year and the person was actually sentecned for no longer than six months, they may seek re-admission.

to the U.S. after inspection and authorization by an officer, they can lose their LPR status.

(5) A person who loses permanent residence status is immediately removable from the United States. They must leave the country as soon as possible or face deportation and removal. In some cases the person may be banned from entering the country for three to seven years, or even permanently.

BENEFITS OF LPR STATUS

On the flip side, in addition to enjoying the freedom to work in the U.S. and travel abroad for a certain period of time without requiring re-admission, a LPR has the right to petition for a spouse or unmarried children to come to the U.S. They may also be eligible for some public benefit programs, depending on where they live. And they may apply for U.S. citizenship after five years of obtaining their LPR status, or less in certain circumstances, such as being married to a U.S. citizen.

An employee who presents LPR status does not need further I-9 re-verification throughout their employment, as they are considered to have permanent status. However, there can be exceptions, for example, such as a condition of probation. LPRs are also strictly required to report any change of address to the USCIS within ten days of any relocation, or face losing their lawful status.

ALIEN NONIMMIGRANT (NI)

A nonimmigrant (NI) alien—those who are admitted as a visitor for a designated period of time and a specific purpose such as tourism, study, diplomacy, or temporary work—may be removed from the U.S. because they either (1) were later found to be inadmissible at the time of entry, (2) have violated a condition of their status in the U.S., or (3) committed other prohibited acts or crimes.

NONIMMIGRANT CRIMINAL CONDUCT

Drug crimes and immigration violations are the most common charges for removal of an NI. Other criminal offenses that warrant removal include rape, sexual abuse of a minor, money laundering, crimes of violence with prison time of at least one year, theft, burglary, kidnapping, child pornography, RICO offenses, human trafficking, fraud in excess of $10,000, forgery, and obstruction of justice.

However, the removal of an NI for criminal conduct applies only after a final conviction or a court enters a formal judgment of guilt. Any adjudication of guilt, where the judge or jury has found the alien guilty or the alien enters a plea of guilty or has admitted sufficient facts to warrant a finding of guilt, will likely be considered a "conviction." A further test of conviction is whether or not a judge has ordered some form of punishment, penalty or restraint on the alien's liberty.

An NI could potentially be removed at any time during or after a probation period because a conviction has been entered. These individuals could also be removed even while an appeal of the conviction is pending.

Further, it is very important to note that if a prior criminal conviction was expunged—destroyed or sealed from the state or federal repository—it does not cancel consideration of that conviction as such for immigration purposes.

The foregoing is not an exhaustive discussion of conditions for the removal of a LPR or an NI. If someone that you employ with permanent or temporary status becomes involved with the law, encourage him or her to obtain the advice of an experienced immigration attorney, immediately. Without this counsel your employee will be swimming in deep water without a lifeline in sight.

IMMIGRANT SAFE PLEAS

The safest advice for immigrants facing criminal charges is to consult with an immigration attorney, in addition to hiring a criminal attorney. Criminal attorneys may not be aware of the affects that certain pleas and sentencing have on immigrants. Criminal attorneys will usually make an effort to keep costs low for their client, and this typically leads to advising that the accused accept deals from the government. While a U.S. citizen can usually accept pleas of "deferred adjudication" so that they can move on with their lives or avoid high attorney's fees, depending on the charge, this may not be acceptable for an immigrant. In immigration terms, deferred adjudication is equal to a conviction.

Immigrants have to be aware of the language of the statutes that they are being charged with, the maximum possible sentence of the charge, and the consequence of incurring too many offenses. While a criminal offense may seem minor to a citizen, it can have grave consequences for immigrants. For instance, a simple conviction for possession of paraphernalia can lead to deportation, while a single marijuana possession under 30 grams falls under the exception to deportability. Additionally, statutes that include language indicating fraud or crimes of moral turpitude can prevent LPRs from renewing their status or naturalizing.

Immigrants are generally safe accepting pleas to misdemeanors that have sentences that are less than one year and say "negligence" somewhere in the statute. However, the safest bet is to consult with an immigration attorney before accepting any pleas or deals.

DACA AND CRIMINAL CONVICTION

Any application for adjustment to an immigrant's status, including application for Deferred Action for Childhood Arrivals (DACA), carries a no tolerance clause for criminal convictions.

Under DACA, the applicant *cannot have a felony conviction,* nor can they have a *significant misdemeanor,* or *multiple misdemeanors.* **Anyone applying for DACA who is even slightly unsure about his or her criminal record, including misdemeanors or any former or current behavior that might be considered a threat to public safety or national security, should not apply without first seeking the advice of a qualified immigration attorney.**

FELONIES AND MISDEMEANORS

What is a felony? A felony is a federal, state, or local offense that is punishable by imprisonment of more than one year. Important to note is that state felony charges vary from state to state.

What is a significant misdemeanor? A misdemeanor can be a federal, state, or local criminal offense that is punishable by imprisonment of one year or less, but more than five days. Misdemeanors include:

- domestic violence;
- sexual abuse or exploitation;
- unlawful possession or use of a firearm;
- drug sales (distribution or trafficking);
- burglary;
- driving under the influence of alcohol or drugs; and,
- any other misdemeanor not listed above for which the person received a jail sentence of more than 90 days—even if they do not actually serve that time in jail.

What are multiple misdemeanors? Multiple misdemeanors in the context of DACA include three or more non-significant misdemeanors. Remember, a misdemeanor is punishable by imprisonment of one year or less, but more than five days.

A minor traffic offense, like driving without a license, will not be considered a misdemeanor for purposes of the DACA process; however, **the entire offense history can be considered along with other facts** to determine whether, under the totality of the circumstances, the individual warrants an exercise of prosecutorial discretion—the wide latitude that prosecutors have

CAUTION: Approvals of exceptional circumstance are very rare.

in determining when, whom, how, and even whether to prosecute apparent violations of the law and the way immigration laws are actually implemented.

If someone has three or more non-significant misdemeanors other than minor traffic offenses, then the **misdemeanors must not occur on the same day nor arise from the same act or scheme of misconduct.** A "scheme of criminal misconduct" generally refers to factors that include time, object and purpose, methods and procedures of the acts, and identity of participants and victims.

The decision whether to defer action in a particular case is an individualized and discretionary one that takes into account the totality of circumstances. Therefore, it is important to note that neither the absence of criminal history nor its presence is necessarily determinative. It is just a factor that will be considered in the exercise of discretion granted to the DHS and USCIS in all DACA applications.

> *The congressmen in both houses have been clear that immigration reform will not be amnesty.*

EXCEPTIONAL CIRCUMSTANCES FOR DACA APPLICANTS

If a DACA applicant falls into one of the three aforementioned categories, but can demonstrate *exceptional circumstances,* he or she may still be able to qualify. Exceptional circumstances are generally noted as those that are beyond the control of the alien, such as battery or extreme cruelty, serious illness, or death to any child or parent of the alien.

HELPING YOUR FRIENDS

It cannot be emphasized enough: Anyone considering DACA must understand that **DACA is a discretionary program.** If you really want to help your friends, let them know that even if they are not automatically barred, but have other questionable characteristics, **the DHS can use a totality of circumstances** and/or threat to public safety analysis in their discretionary determination to award DACA status.

In other words, an individual's history, even without a criminal conviction, arrest or dismissed charges, may be taken into consideration by the DHS to determine whether a person poses a "public safety" or "national security" threat. This includes things like gang membership, drug use or even participation in certain social or political activities that are deemed to threaten the U.S.

This is why it's so important to warn young friends and employees of the long-lasting effects that criminal behavior can have on their future.

To illustrate, if an employee approaches you about a "friend" that is applying for DACA and says that he is particularly concerned about the "friend's" series of driving violations received while using a falsified driver's license, you should strongly suggest that the "friend" conduct their own background check in advance of applying. Tell them that the friend should get records from three sources: the FBI; the State(s); and the court(s). When requesting records, tell them to use "background check" as the purpose for the request, not "immigration."

Also, tell the employee that their "friend" should have an immigration attorney review their entire criminal history, if one exists, including juvenile adjudications before applying. Otherwise, they risk being denied and referred to ICE to be detained and deported.

As the Senate's Gang of Eight is drafting the proposed immigration reform legislation, it appears that it too will have a strong anti-criminal component. Serious criminals will not be eligible for the benefits provided in immigration reform.

REQUESTING CRIMINAL RECORDS

FBI Identification Record. An FBI Identification Record, often referred to as a criminal history record or a rap sheet—Record of Arrests and Prosecutions—is essentially a listing of certain information taken from fingerprint submissions retained by the FBI in connection with arrests and, in some instances, federal employment, naturalization, or military service. Essentially this record will reveal exactly what the DHS will see.

An immigration lawyer should review any rap sheet that turns up. Not only will they note any inconsistencies or red flags, they will be in a better position to advocate for the applicant should it be necessary.

The process of responding to an Identification Record request is generally known as a *criminal background check*. **Only the individual can request a copy of their FBI Identification Record.** The record will include all arrest data that has been obtained not only from fingerprint submissions, but also from disposition reports and other

IMMIGRATION CONSEQUENCES
OF CRIMINAL CONVICTIONS

Deportability

- Controlled Substance Offenses
- Crimes Involving Moral Turpitude
- Multiple Moral Turpitude Convictions
- Aggravated Felonies
- Firearm and Destructive Device Convictions
- Espionage, Sabotage, Treason, and Sedition
- Crimes of Domestic Violence, Stalking, Child Abuse, Child Abandonment or Neglect
- Failure to Register as a Sex Offender
- Violating a Protective Order
- High Speed Flight From an Immigration Checkpoint
- Failure to Register or Falsification of Documents
- Inadmissibility
- Crimes Involving Moral Turpitude
- Controlled Substance Offenses
- Multiple Criminal Convictions
- Conduct-Related Removal (No conviction required)
- Crimes Involving Moral Turpitude
- Controlled Substance Offenses
- Prostitution
- Fraud or Misrepresentation
- Alien Smuggling
- Marriage Fraud
- Human Trafficking
- Money Laundering
- Espionage, Sabotage, and Treason
- Terrorism
- Alien With Physical of Mental Disorder Who Poses Danger to Self of Others
- Unlawful Voters
- Polygamy
- International Child Abduction

information submitted by agencies having criminal justice responsibilities.

In addition to DACA preparation, other common reasons an individual may make this request for personal review is to challenge the information on record, to satisfy a requirement for adopting a child in the U.S. or internationally, or to satisfy a requirement to live, work or travel in a foreign country.

The FBI offers two methods for requesting the FBI Identification Record or proof that a record does not exist. Option 1: Submit the request directly to the FBI (fbi.gov). Option 2: Submit it to an FBI-approved channeler—a private business that has contracted with the FBI to (1) receive the fingerprint submission and relevant data, (2) collect the associated fee(s), (3) electronically forward the fingerprint submission with the necessary information to the FBI CJIS Division for a national criminal history record check, and (4) receive the electronic record check result for dissemination to the requester.

If no record is found, the individual will receive a "no record" response. If there is a criminal history record on file, they will receive their Identification Record—the rap sheet.

Although the FBI includes state rap sheets in their report, FBI reports can be wrong or may not contain enough detail. Therefore, all DACA applicants should also request a rap sheet from any state that may have a record of arrest or conviction.

State Rap Sheet. State rap sheets are maintained by the state's criminal record repository, and each state has a different procedure to obtain criminal records. The individual will need to reference the state website to get the details. The state rap sheet will include any contact he or she may have had with the criminal justice system. If they have ever been arrested, even if the case was dismissed or they were found not guilty, he or she will still have a rap sheet.

Court Records. If an entry turns up on a rap sheet, it is highly recommended that the individual retrieve records from the court where the conviction took place. Do not get a summary of the case; get the entire court file—a complete copy of the record or full disposition from court.

We believe that employers can make a real difference in the lives of their employees and ultimately benefit their company when they demonstrate a willingness to convey proactive warnings or assist in explaining the impact of criminal activity on immigration status. These employers will likely receive in return a more stable workforce and improved employee loyalty—not to mention peace of mind.

CHAPTER 10
OH! OH! OH! OH-BAMACARE!
– BE AWARE OF ITS IMPACT ON
IMMIGRANT WORKFORCES!

"There's not a company in minimum wage industries that isn't looking at cutting back full-time employees to address the cost of the Patient Protection and Affordable Care Act—Obamacare."

The Patient Protection and Affordable Care Act (PPA-CA) became law on March 23, 2010. Also known as the Affordable Care Act or "Obamacare," the requirements of this new law are significant for employers generally, but they are particularly significant for employers with a Latino workforce. As Obamacare rolls out over the coming months and years, there will be numerous issues employers will need to tackle. Meanwhile, we give you the briefest of overviews as to how the PPACA works and a few thoughts on what it means to the Hispanic workforce and their employers.

PPACA OVERVIEW
Obamacare is a very long law. It is over 2000 pages. When you add the regulations, it gets even longer. The number

one issue employers are worried about is the "employer mandate" penalties.

Everyone has heard by now that certain kinds of employers have to offer healthcare insurance coverage to all employees or pay a penalty. Specifically, if an employer has 50 or more full-time employees or their equivalent, the company has to offer affordable insurance coverage to all its full-time employees or pay a penalty. However, where an employee finds the insurance offered by the employer "unaffordable," they could obtain government help, a subsidy, for paying insurance premiums.

Although the details get quite complex as you delve into the law, for the purpose of this overview suffice it to say that many employers will face penalties for not offering qualified coverage.

INCENTIVE FOR UNEMPLOYMENT

While not its intention, the employer mandate under Obamacare has created an incentive for employers to minimize the number of full-time employees they have on their payrolls. This simple fact is *why* you are seeing more borderline employers—those at or near 50 full-time employees—cutting back on the number of full-time workers they hire to sustain their operations and avoid exposure to employer mandate penalties. The fewer full-time employees a company has, the smaller the employer mandate penalties become. This is the logic behind why employers are starting to cut back on full-time employees.

THE CHALLENGE FOR HISPANIC WORKFORCES

The challenge Obamacare presents to employers of primarily Hispanic workforces is two-fold:

(1) Replacing one full-time worker with two part-time workers in order to escape liability for the employer mandate, and

(2) verifying workers under an almost certain expectation that immigration reform will require employers to begin using the E-Verify online system.

To put this into perspective, let's suppose you have an employee that presently works 40 hours a week and you decide to let that employee go because you want to replace him with two part-time employees at 20 hours to meet the employer mandate. Although your goal is to limit your employer liability under Obamacare, you soon learn that replacing one 40-hour employee who has verified his work authorization with two part-time employees, who each must pass verification, is not as easy as you thought it would be. In fact, it is particularly difficult because your company participates in E-Verify. Thus, you need to weigh the pros and cons to determine whether the effort is worth anything to your organization.

Undocumented workers do not qualify for insurance coverage under Obamacare.

E-VERIFY REQUIREMENTS: NOT LOOSENING AT A TIME WHEN MORE LABOR IS NEEDED

Employers with Hispanic employees get hit twice with regulations from the Obama Administration. One law encourages the doubling (or tripling) of a workforce, while a second law simultaneously demands labor be put through a filter that keeps most of the ready, willing, and able employees away from the very employers that wish they could hire them.

Although the current use of E-Verify in traditionally Hispanic industries such as hospitality, farming and manufacturing, for example, is low, the time is coming when ALL employers will be required to use it, as it appears that E-Verify will be a mandatory component of any immigration reform bill that makes it into law.

Meanwhile, employers trying to follow the law and screen applicants for lawful work authorization—with or without E-Verify—will begin to feel the affects once they begin hunting for two employees instead of one.

OBAMACARE: MUCH ADO ABOUT NOTHING FOR HISPANIC LABOR

Even if an employer is prepared to offer employees insurance under the employer mandate, this does not help their undocumented employees that are not entitled to accept such an offer—essentially making Obamacare a total non-issue for undocumented workers. You should be aware that the proposed immigration reform released in mid-April 2013 will place its main benefactors (those individuals who will phase out of unlawful status into some new provisionally lawful status) in the same category as undocumented workers. This should help employers with large Hispanic workforces because they will receive the benefit of a new, lawful labor force without Obamacare's requirement to offer full-time employees within that labor force health insurance.

Under Obamacare, the biggest incentive for any an individual to obtain employer insurance (aside from having coverage) is to avoid paying an IRS penalty at the end of the year for not having insurance coverage. But most, if not all, undocumented workers do not currently file income tax returns!

Without filing an income tax return, there is no way the IRS can penalize an individual for not carrying insurance coverage throughout the year. Thus, Obamacare is a non-starter for much of the current, undocumented Hispanic labor pool and their employers.

On the other hand, for documented Hispanic workers, Obamacare does little to actually help them, either. The law does not reduce nor control the price of insurance. And while the employer is obligated to provide "affordable" care, if the employee finds it unaffordable—based on the law's proscribed income calculation—they face two unattractive options: they (1) must apply for government assistance or (2) personally pay a penalty tax for being uninsured.

Keep in mind that health insurance coverage has been typically prohibitively expensive for employees in low-wage industries that are traditionally staffed by Hispanic employees making minimum wage or close to it. Therefore, paying for healthcare is generally considered a low priority for those employees who do not see the value of giving up

good portions of their paychecks to pay for insurance—
something most perceive as a luxury.

> *Not offering insurance is not what gets a company in trouble,*
> *rather, under Obamacare, not offering "affordable" insur-*
> *ance will.*

Perhaps one of the most misunderstood things about
Obamacare is that not offering insurance is not the great-
est cost. Paying the penalties for full-time employees who
obtain government help in paying for his or her coverage is
and can add up to significant expense.

For example, if an employee cannot technically afford
the employer's plan—as defined in the law by a percentage
of total household income—but wants to avoid a personal penalty tax for not being insured, they can apply for a
government subsidy and get coverage. When the employee
applies for federal assistance in paying for the healthcare
offered through the employer, the employer pays a penalty.
We believe that this can escalate quite quickly if the workforce is primarily minimum wage because the employer
pays the penalty for each worker that chooses the government subsidy.

Notwithstanding, we predict that most Hispanic employees will not take advantage of the available subsidies
and will simply opt out of the employer plan—seeing the
personal tax penalty as the worse of two evils. There are
two things to consider and that lead us to this conclusion:
(1) Hispanic workforces are very distrusting of the federal
government, generally, and (2) the application for federal

subsidy is pages long! The second fact alone will probably intimidate many Hispanic employees, and they will not apply for a subsidy.

Finally, where an employer offers affordable insurance coverage but an employee rejects it and does not apply for a federal subsidy—because the personal tax penalty is less than the employee's contribution would be—the employer is off the hook for any employer mandate penalty.

★ ★ ★

A FINAL WORD

Economists, demographers and other experts who have studied the potential impact of immigration reform are uncertain of its effects on economic recovery, but most remain optimistic and project that it will have positive effects on both employees and employers.

Economics aside, immigration reform will certainly benefit individual immigrants and their families. Improved work conditions provide stability. Stability promotes integration and assimilation. And, integration and assimilation increase opportunities for individuals and societies at large. In addition, immigrants with legal status may become more likely to invest in education for themselves and their children because they would feel more secure and settled.

The last large-scale immigration overhaul—the Immigration Reform and Control Act, or IRCA—occurred in 1986. At the time, 2.7 million immigrants were legalized. Today, we're looking at legalizing approximately 11 million undocumented people who are currently living (and working) in the United States. Several studies reveal that under the IRCA, Latin American immigrants who secured green cards—Lawful Permanent Residence—saw their wages increase between 6 percent and 13 percent, according to a February 3, 2013, article in the Wall Street Journal. The payoff for society at large, when people earn higher wages and those who work off the books come onto the tax roll, is not insignificant. According to the Social Security Administration's "suspense file," there are billions of dollars in contributions to payroll taxes and wage withholdings that can't be matched to real persons. This suggests that there was a lot of false documentation in use in the U.S. workforce. Although most employers do not knowingly hire undocumented employees, they are unlikely to detect if someone presents fake identification unless they use the electronic worker-eligibility system, E-Verify. And even that is not foolproof.

As illustrated in *The Gringo's Guide to Hispanics in the Workplace,* it is very easy for an undocumented individual to cross the border and acquire very sophisticated fake documentation within a few weeks, for a reasonable amount of money. Add to that, the use of E-Verify is mandatory only in some states and for federal contractors, leaving many employers to their own discretion to verify identification submitted with the employee's I-9 form. And as mentioned before, E-Verify is not 100 percent reliable.

There is no practical way to know exactly how many current workers will come clean under immigration reform—especially in lower-wage workforces. But regardless, companies with large Hispanic workforces will encounter significant opportunities, changes, and challenges.

Forewarned is forearmed—"To be prepared is half the victory." We trust that the foregoing content has prepared, enlightened and enriched all employers, and possibly their "friends," as we ring in a new era of immigration reform.

If you have questions or comments about the Hispanic workforce, or other Hispanic issues you may encounter, please email us at **jmonty@montyramirezlaw.com or smonty@montyramirezlaw.com.**

We encourage you to reference our Suggested Reading List, and invite you to visit our website *www.MontyRamirezLaw.com* for updated information, articles, links, educational materials, and events.

Lastly, should you desire to hire our firm, we represent employers and employees across the United States in immigration law.

Suggested Reading

Immigration Wars: Forging an American Solution, Jeb Bush and Clint Bolick, Threshold Editions; First Edition, New York (March 2013).

Los Republicanos: Why Hispanics and Republicans Need Each Other, Leslie Sanchez and Palgrave MacMillan, New York (2007).

HisPanic: Why Americans Fear Hispanics in the U.S., Geraldo Rivera, Celebra, New York (2008).

Think and Grow Rich: A Latino Choice, Lionel Sosa and Napoleon Hill Foundation, Ballantine Books, New York (May 2006).

Spanish Twins: Start Speaking Spanish on the Construction Site with Words You Already Know, Bradley Hartmann, (October 2011).

Acknowledgements

We wish to express our sincere gratitude to the clients of Monty & Ramirez LLP and to the employees of our clients. Every single day you give us new opportunities to delve into exciting nuances of the law, and we are grateful to work with you and for you as the law changes with time and progress.

We also wish to thank the attorneys and staff of Monty & Ramirez LLP. This book could not have come together without your dedication and commitment, and we are extremely proud that you are part of our team.

For further information about the law firm of Monty & Ramirez LLP please visit our website at www.Monty RamirezLaw.com.

Bonus Material
FOR FRIENDS OF GRINGOS

As the grandchildren of immigrants, we have a personal interest in helping others who, like our great grandparents, left their country in search of opportunity in a foreign land. The United States of America is a nation built by immigrants who arrived on its shores from around the world and who willingly took risks and accepted sacrifices for the privileges of "life, liberty and the pursuit of happiness." It is our dream that many journeys might be improved through the offer of a helping hand—guidance from a trusted counselor and the support of friends and families.

From restaurants to farming, carpet installation to roofing and from business, technology, medicine, and education, our society relies on Hispanics for knowledgeable, skillful, talented, and industrious workers and professionals. Without a doubt, Hispanics from all walks of life make important contributions that impact our country's greater good.

There is nothing more frightening than living or working in the shadows, with the fear of being deported and separated from family and loved ones. As we write this book, many Americans are working at the forefront to pass immigration reform—and we thank them. Still, what undocumented workers and their children need right now to help them on their road to legal certainty is your helping hand in passing along information contained in this bonus material.

> *CAUTION: Employers should always refrain from discussing an employee's immigration status with an employee.*

That being said, we hope the following information may be very helpful to you, your friends, neighbors, and the communities where we live, work and play.

Gracias,
Jacob and Sarah

PART 1
COMMON QUESTIONS FROM THE COMMUNITY AT LARGE

Q. I have been asked to provide a letter of support for my neighbor, Mr. Garcia, who is undocumented and is fighting his deportation. He is a great guy but I am not sure what to say in the letter.

A. Before attempting to write the letter, sit down and gather your thoughts. The more specific examples you can produce, the better you will be able to write your letter effectively. Again, keep in mind that this will be a letter written for a neighbor or a friend, not an employee.

1) Introduction - Give your name, profession and indicate the purpose of your letter. State your relationship to the family and the length of time that you have known them.

   My name is John Smith, and I am a business owner. I am writing this letter in support of Mr. Joaquin Garcia. I have been Mr. Garcia's neighbor for 10 years.

2) Describe the positive attributes of Mr. Garcia's character. Discuss why he is a good neighbor. Specific examples are very valuable.

Mr. Garcia is a hardworking, law-abiding man. He is also a good neighbor and a valuable member of our community.

Hurricane Ike hit our town a few years ago and we were without electricity for almost five days. Mr. Garcia and his wife led the other neighbors in making sure that we were getting food and water to the elderly people in our neighborhood.

3) Describe the hardship the Garcia family would suffer if Mr. Garcia is forced to return to Mexico and be separated from his family. Again, specific examples will make your letter more valuable.

Mr. Garcia and his wife have a great family. They have two children: Juan and Maria. Both students are honor students in high school. Mr. Garcia is the main breadwinner for his family. If he is deported, I know that his family would suffer extreme economic and emotional hardship. Additionally, if he is deported, his children may have to interrupt their education to help their mother make-ends-meet.

4) Conclusion. Reiterate your support and offer your telephone number or email address should any further information be required.

I believe that Mr. Garcia has been an excellent member of the community he should be allowed to remain in the United States. Please count on my cooperation should you require further information. My telephone number is 281-493-5529. Additionally, I can be reached by email at sdm@montypartners.com

Q. What is a deferred action for undocumented immigrants?

A. On June 15, 2012, the Obama Administration announced that a new program had been created to offer special relief for the estimated two million individuals who were brought to the U.S. as youngsters. The program is known as Deferred Action for Childhood Arrivals, or DACA. There are many benefits to those young people who pursue deferred action, but it is important to understand that there are also many responsibilities. Remember, there are dire consequences for immigrants who commit crimes.

All undocumented immigrants in the United States may apply for deferred action relief from immediate deportation.

- Deferred action is a temporary administrative relief from deportation, available to individuals who do not hold legal papers.
- Deferred action has been around a long time.
- A deferred action authorizes a non-U.S. citizen to temporarily remain in the United States.
- Anyone granted a deferred action may apply for a work permit.
- A grant of deferred action does not provide a direct path to lawful permanent residency or U.S. citizenship.
- Deferred actions fall under the U.S. Department of Homeland Security.
- All deferred actions are granted on a case-by-case basis.

Part 2
COMMON QUESTIONS ABOUT DACA

Q. I have just applied for DACA and I cannot wait to get my work permit! However, I am currently working using a different name. I feel a little guilty that all this time I have been lying about my name and immigration status.

Should I tell my supervisor that I will soon get my work permit with my real name? I have a good relationship with my supervisor.

A. Your immigration status is personal private information and generally you should not share this with anyone other than your attorney. If you disclose this information to your employer or anyone at work, you run the risk of being fired.

Employers have a legal responsibility under current U.S. immigration laws to make sure that they do not employ unauthorized workers. Even though you will be eligible to work legally if you receive an approval of deferred action and your Employment Authorization Document (EAD), if you tell your employer that you will be applying for DACA, you are essentially telling them that you are not currently eligible to work legally in the U.S. When your employer learns that you are ineligible to work in the U.S., he or she will have a legal obligation to fire you or risk breaking the law.

- You are not required to tell your employer that you are applying for DACA,
- Nor should your boss or supervisor ask you if you are applying for DACA.
- If they do, you should tell them you are not comfortable answering that question.

This can be a hard situation, especially if you have a friendly relationship with your boss. In fact, you might be excited about the prospect and feel tempted to tell him or her that you are applying for DACA. **Do not do this.** If you share this information with your employer, you risk losing your job.

Q. Should I ask my boss for documents that help prove that I have lived continuously in the U.S. since June 15, 2007? I really do not have much proof that I have been living here after I graduated in 2006. Once I started working after graduation, I was paid in cash. The only thing I can think of is asking my employers to write letters verifying my employments.

A. Proof of continuous residency in the U.S. is required when applying for DACA and for other immigration benefits. Generally, if you can prove that you have been in the U.S. without having to ask your employer for an employment verification letter, you should.

There are plenty other more acceptable documents you can use such as school records, letters, report cards, immunization records, rent receipts or utility bills, bank transactions, even traffic tickets. Basically you can use anything that was issued by an organization that has your name and the date it was produced to prove continuous residency. However, if you must get information from your employer, such as a letter confirming your employment, you have to be very careful about how you ask.

- Do not mention that your request for information is for immigration purposes.
- Make your request in a way that does not alert your employer to your immigration status.
- Do not tell your employer that you are applying for DACA or any other immigration benefit.
- Simply request a letter or other document that confirm the dates that you have been employed.
- If your employer asks why you are making this request, answer that you would rather not say why and that it relates to a private matter.

Q. If I have received my employment authorization document (EAD), may I apply for any job?

A. Yes. After you are hired by an employer, but within the first three days of work, the employer should ask you to complete an I-9 employment eligibility verification form and to present documents that prove you are eligible to work legally in the U.S.

At that time, you can present your EAD. Your employer might make a copy of your EAD to keep with the record.

Q. When I interview for a job, do I need to tell the person interviewing me that I applied for DACA or why I was eligible to receive an EAD?

A. No. You do not need to tell your employer that you received an EAD through the DACA program, and the employer should not ask.

Q. I just got my DACA application approved and I was issued an employment authorization card (EAD). Should I show the EAD to my employer or will the government let my employer know that I can legally work?

A. U.S. Citizenship and Immigration Services (USCIS) *will not* alert your employer that you have received an employment authorization document (EAD). So if you do not tell your employer that you have received an EAD, it is unlikely that the employer will know you have one.

If you do show your EAD to your employer and the name and birth date on the EAD are different from the name and birth date on the I-9 form your employer has on file for you, the employer is required to have you fill out a new I-9 form.

Your employer is also required to have you complete a new I-9 form if your old I-9 form contains a Social Security Number (SSN) that is different from your new SSN.

Further, your employer is required to have you complete a new I-9 form if you check-marked an immigration or citizenship status or provided an "alien number" on your old form that doesn't match the status or alien number that's indicated on your EAD. For example, if your original I-9 form has a checkmark next to "A citizen of the United States," they must complete a new Form I-9.

Typically, once you are hired and have completed the I-9 or E-Verify process, your employer *should not* ask to see your EAD or any other identity or employment eligibility verification document again until the time a document you provided expires.

Q. Now that I have been granted Deferred Adjudication and I have an employment authorization card, should I correct information on my W-4 form?

A. Yes. It is important that all the information on your W-4 form be correct. It helps the government know how long you have been working and ensures that your contributions to the Social Security Trust Fund are recorded. It is important to have your record straight so that you can get credit for all the time you worked in the U.S.

Q. I have just finished high school and I know that I qualify for DACA but I would rather wait to file for residency when immigration reform is passed because DACA does not provide a direct path to citizenship.

A. It is true. DACA does not provide a direct path to citizenship. But it does provide protection against deportation and you will get an employment authorization document (EAD). Once you have an EAD, you can apply for a driver's license.

So, while it looks as if immigration reform will pass, we do not know for certain that it will pass and if it does pass there is no guarantee that there will be a direct path to citizenship for you. But meanwhile, right now you are driving without a license—which is against the law. You may even be working without permission using fake documents—which is also against the law. DACA is not perfect, but it is a good vehicle to get safe, and get legal now.

PART 3
IMMIGRATION REFORM CHECKLIST: GET READY FOR POSSIBLE REFORM

Here is a helpful checklist to share with your immigrant friends and neighbors so that they can get ready for a possible immigration reform. Discussing these *ten suggestions* will go a long way toward helping them prepare and be ready. It will also be a great way to help strengthen your community.

1. **Learn to use the web to access information regarding immigration reform.** The best online resource available is the U.S. Customs and Immigration Service (USCIS) website [www.uscis.gov]. But be careful as you surf the web—there are non-governmental sites that provide incorrect information or may attempt to sell you services you do not need, or worse, sell you services that will actually hurt your chances of becoming legal.

   If you think you are on a government site, you will always see the following ending www dot site name dot GOV. Remember the government will never contact via email to ask you for money.

2. **Consult a reputable immigration attorney or a reputable non-profit organization with your immigration questions.** Remember, immigration law is very complex—probably the most complex area of law today. You should talk to a professional, not to your neighbor or mother-in-law. Get the facts from a reliable source. A great source is the American Immigration Lawyers Association, found at http://www.ailalawyer.com/

3. **Get your evidence together to prove physical presence in the U.S.** It's never too early to begin assembling all the information you can find that proves you have lived in the United States for as long as you have. That information may include:

   - Educational records
     - Contact your local school district for a copy of your school transcript. These records are solid evidence that you were in the U.S.
     - School documents signed by parents present evidence that they were present in U.S.
   - Financial records
     - Tax records. If you have been filing your taxes, you can request a transcript of your tax records online at http://www.irs.gov/Individuals/Order-a-Transcript, or call 1-800-908-9946
     - Bank records. If you do not have paper statements, you can request copies from your bank.
     - Property records
     - Lease agreements

- Car titles
- Credit card records
- Cell phone bills or records
- Medical bills and prescriptions. These are excellent proof that you were in the U.S. as each bill and prescription has the name of the patient and date the service was rendered.
- Biographical Records
  - Google search: "Your Name + Vital Statics + Texas (Your State)"
  - Birth certificate
  - Make sure you have a copy of your birth certificate. If you do not have a copy of your birth certificate, request a certified copy from your home country or visit your nearest consulate now.
  - Birth Certificates of USC Family Members [Google: "Name + Vital Statics + Texas (Your State)"]
  - Grants of Deferred Action – I-821 Approvals. If you have children who have been granted DACA, make sure that you get a copy of their receipt in your file.
  - Marriage certificate if you were married in the U.S.
  - Divorce decrees (U.S.)
  - Expired U.S. driver's licenses
  - Copies of traffic ticket(s) can be used to show that you were present in the U.S. (Make sure to pay those tickets before applying for a benefit.)

- Immigration records
  - Has a family member filed a immigration petition for you? Get a copy of the receipt or approval notice.
  - Deportation orders. Yes, even these are helpful to prove that you have been present in the U.S. Make sure to share this information with your immigration attorney and discuss any derogatory history.
  - "Matricula Consular." There is a date on each card that proves you were present in the U.S. when you received it.
  - Foreign passport. A copy of the stamped passport showing your entry is excellent evidence that you were present in the U.S.
  - Denied petitions. If a case did not go right and you have a copy of the application, this is good evidence that you were in the U.S.
  - Lastly, store all your records in a safe place. Do not give the originals to anyone, not even your attorney, unless you have another copy to keep in storage for yourself.

4. **Prepare to pass an English competency examination.** You may have to prove that you can read, write and speak English. You may also have to pass an American Civics Exam as well. But do not worry! Remember, immigration examiners are not English teachers and will not have a lot of time to spend testing you. They simply want to make sure that you understand and can converse in basic English. A good way to prepare for

this is by studying the exam that is used for naturalization purposes. It will probably be the same exam.

What questions will the examiner ask? Not hard ones. The will simply speak to you while they are reviewing your application.

What questions will be on the application?

- What is your address?
- Are you married or single?
- How many children do you have?

So while learning English is a good idea, those that are finding it difficult should **keep in mind that this is one exam that you can study for and pass.**

The USCIS has done a great job assembling lots of information that you can access for free! Start studying now. The reading and writing vocabulary lists are not long and can be memorized. Find more information at http://www.uscis.gov/portal/site/uscis/citizenship.

5. **Always tell the truth.** Do not lie to the United States Government. While in many countries it is common to tell a lie—everyone does it to get anything done—this is NOT the way things work in the U.S.A.

- Do not lie to obtain any benefit. Misrepresentation or lying to obtain any benefit can be prosecuted as a crime.
- Do not lie to your attorney. This is not a smart thing to do. Your attorney needs to really understand your

matter. If you lie to your attorney you are just wasting your time and money, and you could be compromising your future.

- Do not create evidence. If you do not qualify for a benefit, then you do not qualify. Creating evidence is considered fraud and fraud is a crime. The U.S. government is out to stamp out fraud.

- Do not lie to yourself. Sometimes we want to avoid unpleasant things that have happened in the past and act as if they did not happen. Know that this is dangerous. The truth will really set you free and make sure that you remain out of trouble.

6. **Get a certified copy of your criminal record.** If you have committed or pled guilty to a crime you need to get that record and have it analyzed by an immigration attorney with experience in representing individuals with criminal histories before you apply for any immigration benefit. Make sure that you obtain every single page of your criminal record. A print-out is not enough. To obtain your criminal record you can Google: "your name + county + criminal record." Do not file without a review from an immigration attorney that has experience in criminal matters.

7. **Get translations of entire documents submitted in foreign languages.** If you plan to provide a document in a foreign language, make sure that the entire document you submit has been *properly* translated.

8. **File your taxes.** If you have not yet filed a tax return to the U.S. Internal Revenue Service, make sure you

do so, for this year at least. It is important to read the mood of the country. Filing your taxes is the way you show that you are part of the solution for America.

9. **Continue to practice self-sufficiency and self-reliance.** As an immigrant, you know that public benefits are not available to you, nor will they be should immigration reform become a reality. Get ready for the expenses you will be facing. Start saving up money to pay for government filing fees and attorney fees.

10. **Continue to exhibit outstanding behavior in your community.** Remember, immigrants will always pay twice for any wrongdoing. Continue to be an example to the rest of society. Avoid situations that can result in trouble with the law. Understand that "Driving While Under the Influence of Alcohol" can compromise your future in the United States. Diffuse tense situations at home. A conviction of domestic abuse not only hurts your family, but also compromises your future with them in the United States.

Should need further assistance please contact us at 713.289.4546 or smonty@montyramirezlaw.com.

CPSIA information can be obtained at www.ICGtesting.com
Printed in the USA
LVOW060305230513

334967LV00001B/2/P